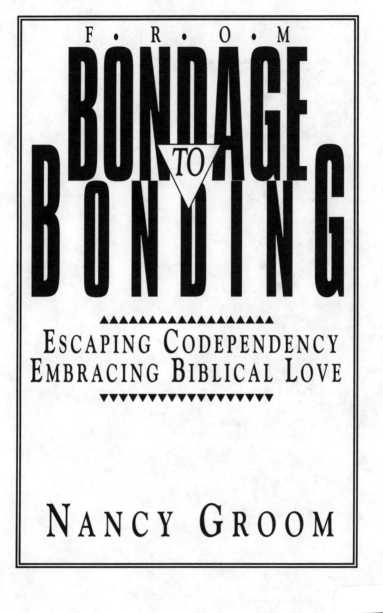

F·R·O·M

BONDAGE TO BONDING

▲▲▲▲▲▲▲▲▲▲▲▲▲▲▲▲▲▲

ESCAPING CODEPENDENCY
EMBRACING BIBLICAL LOVE

▼▼▼▼▼▼▼▼▼▼▼▼▼▼▼▼

NANCY GROOM

NAVPRESS
A MINISTRY OF THE NAVIGATORS
P.O. BOX 35001, COLORADO SPRINGS, COLORADO 80935

The Navigators is an international Christian organization. Jesus Christ gave His followers the Great Commission to go and make disciples (Matthew 28:19). The aim of The Navigators is to help fulfill that commission by multiplying laborers for Christ in every nation.

NavPress is the publishing ministry of The Navigators. NavPress publications are tools to help Christians grow. Although publications alone cannot make disciples or change lives, they can help believers learn biblical discipleship, and apply what they learn to their lives and ministries.

© 1991 by Nancy Groom
All rights reserved. No part of this publication may be reproduced in any form without written permission from NavPress, P.O. Box 35001, Colorado Springs, CO 80935.
Library of Congress Catalog Card Number: 90-64221
ISBN 08910-96205

Third printing, 1992

Unless otherwise identified, all Scripture in this publication is from the *Holy Bible: New International Version* (NIV). Copyright © 1973, 1978, 1984, International Bible Society. Used by permission of Zondervan Bible Publishers. Another version used is *The Living Bible* (TLB), © 1971 owned by assignment by the Illinois Regional Bank N.A. (as trustee), used by permission of Tyndale House Publishers, Inc., Wheaton, IL 60189.

Printed in the United States of America

CONTENTS

To my father and mother,
Edward and Harriet Venema,
with love and gratitude
for who they are
and for all they have done for me.

AUTHOR

Nancy Groom taught junior high English and Bible for several years after her graduation from Calvin College in Grand Rapids, Michigan. She married in 1970 and became a full-time mother in 1971. Her writing career began in 1983 as a writer and editor of Sunday school, catechism, and Christian day school curriculum materials. Her first book, *Married Without Masks,* was published in 1989.

Nancy's leadership in Bible studies, support groups, conferences, and codependency workshops over the years has emerged from her own ongoing struggle toward healing from codependency. It has also kept her in touch with a broad spectrum of other people grappling with the issues she addresses in this book and its companion workbook.

Nancy lives with her husband, Bill, and their son, Christopher, in Miami, Florida.

PREFACE:
PROMISES FOR THE JOURNEY

❦

Blessed are those whose strength is in [God],
who have set their hearts on pilgrimage.
(Psalm 84:5)

We were having lunch together, just the four of us, comrades walking the hard road toward repentance and healing from codependency. These members of my support group for families of substance abusers had become dear to me during my rough first six months of disentangling from enmeshed relationships. Looking for some light at the end of my tunnel, I asked Joanne, a veteran traveler on this road, how long she'd been involved in her recovery process.

Her answer dismayed me: "Oh, about ten years, I guess." Ten years! I was hoping she'd say ten months! Then she added, "I figure I'll probably be struggling with these issues the rest of my life."

Oh, no! I thought. *I don't plan to stay in this misery that long. I want to finish this process and get on with the rest of my life. Ten years!*

My dismay ran deep, but gradually the blessing side of what Joanne had said began to sink in. If she could calmly tell me she'd been through it all and had not only survived but had found serenity in the journey, maybe there was hope for me after all—not the hope I'd had of finishing soon, but hope that I wouldn't be destroyed along the way.

More than that, as I began to taste God's comfort and presence in exchanging my old codependent strategies one by one for the terrors of grace, I grew to hope I would not just survive but would actually find Life.

That is what has happened—is happening—to me. As I proceed through the sometimes sorrowful, often confusing, almost-always uncertain process of change from codependency to mutual interdependence in my relationships, I have fallen in love with life—God's own Life flowing into me and through me into the lives of people around me. I identify and rejoice with the Apostle Paul: "We are hard pressed on every side, but not crushed; perplexed, but not in despair; persecuted, but not abandoned; struck down, but not destroyed" (2 Corinthians 4:8-9). Despite the sorrow, confusion, and uncertainty interspersing my good days, deep in my soul is the unshakable knowledge that I am precious to God and adequate to the task of loving well. I wouldn't trade this Life for any amount of "safety" or "predictability" that codependency once offered me.

Nor would I trade the friends I've made along the way, friends who support, encourage, pray for, cry with, confront, inspire, and laugh with me. I can't do without their help to see what I can't see alone—myself as I really am. God created us for community. My support group has been both a lifeline to reality and a pipeline of God's grace to me throughout my continuing years of return to His design for living.

I still haven't been walking this road for as long as Joanne had been when I first asked her that question. But I'm past my six-months-into-recovery delusion that I'll ever have it all together and be finished battling my codependent inclinations. I've made some progress; I don't act codependently all the time in every relationship. But perhaps the most wonderful change of all is that I no longer feel so compulsive about becoming perfect. I'm in process, and God's not finished with me yet. I don't always understand or enjoy what He's doing, but I'm more and more willing to trust His plan for me.

Someone has said, "Everyone wants to grow, but no one wants to change," yet the two are inseparable. As God calls you and me to the discomfort of change for the purpose of growth, He promises us His presence and the reproduction in us of His Son's life and character along the way. If your heart is turned toward Him, you can have great courage as you embark on your journey out of codependency and into biblical love. It's going to have its difficult seasons, but when we get Home, we'll unanimously agree it was infinitely worth whatever it cost. May God's grace surround your pilgrimage!

ACKNOWLEDGMENTS

Several people have contributed to the writing of this book, blessing and shaping me with their faithful love.

I wish to thank my husband, Bill, whose courage to come alive and whose godly strength on my behalf offer me deep joy and contentment. You're loving me well, dear friend, and I'm glad we're sharing the adventure of becoming one.

And to our son, Christopher, who walks his own journey with integrity and who put up with a fair amount of neglect as I completed this manuscript: I love you, Chris. You bring me great pleasure just by being who you are.

I'm also grateful to Lottie Hillard, who models the grace of a persistent love and a dogged commitment to my good, even when it hurts. You've taught me much about bold love, Lottie, and I treasure our friendship.

Dr. Dan Allender is another person to whom I owe deep gratitude, both for his teaching and for his personal kindness to me, which have blessed my life in countless ways. Thank you, Dan, for your contributions to this manuscript and for the privilege of being your friend.

I am fortunate to have many other friends who consistently pray for and engage with me: Maryanne, Dan and Joyce, Robin, Patricia, Mari, Dick and Pat, Julie, Jack and Judy, Kristine, Jody, and Melinda. Your courage in abandoning your codependency and your love as I abandon mine, fellow pilgrims, inspire me more than you can know.

To my beloved and gifted editor, Traci Mullins, I owe an incalculable debt for her patience and her profound insight into what I wanted to say. You are wonderful, Traci, and I thank God for our friendship and your expertise.

The Father has been good beyond my deserving. Without Him there is no light, no life, no love, but at His right hand are pleasures forevermore. I've tasted His pleasure, and I am being changed. Praise God from whom all blessings flow!

PART ONE

WHAT DOES BONDAGE LOOK LIKE?

1

CODEPENDENCY: A SELF-FOCUSED WAY OF LIFE

❦

Codependency has a fuzzy definition because it is a gray,
fuzzy condition. It is complex, theoretical, and difficult
to completely define in one or two sentences.
MELODY BEATTIE
Codependent No More

Nothing was working anymore. Not the cheerful facade, not the furtive manipulating, not the dogged attempts at normalcy, not even the desperate prayers that God *do* something. "It's hopeless," Jenny's inner voice concluded. "You might as well give up."

Jenny sat on the edge of her bed and glanced around. Her wedding picture with Brad smiled at her, and she wondered with a cynical laugh, "How could the promises have so betrayed us both?" The photos of the children caught in spontaneous play pierced Jenny's heart with regret and guilt now that things were so different, so awful. After twenty-six years of marriage and the raising of two daughters, Jenny felt numb and out of touch with life. Her world was closing in on her.

Brad had just returned to the store after supper. It was the same old story. He'd come home angry and half drunk again. Even when no one else could tell, Jenny knew. She also knew with nervous certainty how things would go when Brad came home again at 9:30 that night. The sale he'd planned was not going well, and his drinking would surely escalate.

The fallout of Brad's anger had landed, as usual, on the family. At supper he'd complained about the food, fumed about the broken dishwasher, criticized Jenny's housework—and all the while Jenny nervously apologized. Their daughter Jodie, a high school senior, seemed immune to her father's condition and comments. After supper she'd retreated again to her bedroom without a word.

"At least Melinda is away at college, away from the responsibility she always took for her father's drinking," Jenny sighed to herself. She missed Melinda—even envied her—but she was glad her daughter could escape the craziness. Soon Jodie would be gone, too, and then Jenny would be alone with Brad. When that realization occasionally broke through her usual wall of denial, Jenny's heart constricted with sudden dismay.

In a way, the failure of Brad's sale that particular day wasn't the issue at all; he drank just as much when a sale went well. Jenny knew things were getting worse, but she could see no way out.

The pain was catching up with her. Troubleshooting the business and social disasters caused by Brad's drinking over the years had wounded Jenny more than she realized. With the familiar knots tightening in her stomach, she recalled the spoiled dinner parties, the missed holiday celebrations, the nights she had bundled her young girls out of bed and into the car to rescue Brad, too drunk to drive, from the downtown bar. She frowned and shook her head as she recalled her explanation: "Daddy's just sick; he'll be better soon." She wondered if they had believed her.

"What choice did I have?" she asked herself. "I couldn't let anyone see him drunk. What if the pastor had found out and Brad couldn't be a deacon anymore? What if Brad had an accident and killed someone?" At the time it seemed necessary to "save Brad from himself." But now, after years of coping with his erratic and increasingly volatile behavior, Jenny was feeling used, unappreciated, trapped, even a little angry.

In fact, Jenny was very angry, though much of her anger was unconscious. Terrified that her anger might cause Brad to abandon her, she refused to experience that anger. She wouldn't let herself feel angry at her daughters, either, though they were demanding and unappreciative of her efforts to please them. And, of course, no one except her closest sister knew how uncontrolled Brad's drinking had become, or how chaotic Jenny's life was because of it. She was angry, to be sure, but her anger had taken the form of martyrdom, silent withdrawal from Brad and the children, social isolation, increasing depression, and a camouflaged resentment that was rapidly settling into chronic bitterness—not just toward Brad but toward life in general. She felt like a puppet with its strings hanging out for just anyone to pull.

"That's it," Jenny thought bitterly as the image played across her mind. "I'm everybody's marionette, yanked around day after day, dancing to whatever tune someone else wants to play. What about my tune? Why is no one meeting my needs? Will this nightmare never end?"

ADDICTION IN TODAY'S SOCIETY

Jenny, like thousands of others caught in unhealthy relationships, was finally becoming desperate about the way things were going. Marriage to an alcoholic generates overwhelming emotions that are difficult to admit, even to oneself—anger, resentment, paralyzing fear, self-pity, and confusion. Alcoholic homes breed negative attitudes and behavior, and people and families are destroyed by what goes on there.

But other situations besides alcoholism cause similar feelings of helplessness. Living with an out-of-control child (who may be abusing drugs, sex, or alcohol), a chronically ill or terminally ill family member, a compulsive eater, spender, worker, or gambler, an abuser (physically, emotionally, or sexually), a sex addict, or a mentally disabled relative or close friend can produce the same confusion and despair. Though some compulsions (like overeating or workaholism) may appear less destructive than alcoholism or drug addiction, people who love the overeater or workaholic can suffer as much damage as those related to alcoholics or addicts. The helplessness feels the same, regardless of the dysfunction.

Some people feel out of control and confused about their lives but can't understand why. Although their lives seem more or less normal, they find themselves overwhelmed when they shouldn't be, angry out of proportion to their experiences, depressed without identifiable reason. The compulsions mentioned above may not be occurring in their lives at the time, yet negative feelings persist.

Perhaps it's because one or more of those compulsive situations existed in their family of origin (the family in which they were raised). The effects are often handed down. Children who grew up in a family environment with addiction, compulsion, or abuse are profoundly affected as adults in ways many don't realize. The increasing number of people in support organizations like Adult Children of Alcoholics indicates that emotions damaged in childhood don't go away if left unattended—they just go underground. Scenarios from the family of origin often repeat themselves in the adult lives of children who grew up there, despite those children's determination that "It will never happen to me." One's childhood with an alcoholic, abusive, or emotionally neglectful parent shapes that person's self-image and expectation of "normal" family life. People move unthinkingly toward repeating (and trying to correct) what they have experienced, even when they believe something else would be better for them.

The increase of addiction and compulsivity in today's society has far-reaching and terrible effects. It has brought on an exponential increase in family problems, such as child abuse (physical, emotional, and sexual), addiction-induced financial collapse, loss of nurturing for children, loss of intimacy in marriages, pre- and extramarital affairs, and a host of other related difficulties. But also, an unprecedented number of children have come out of those dysfunctional homes unable to relate to others in healthy ways. Thus the problems of addiction and its inevitable destructive consequences are multiplying at an alarming rate, and the resources for dealing with these problems are often inadequate and ineffective.

ADDICTION IN TODAY'S CHURCH

Where is Christ's Church in all of this? Are addictions and their accompanying demons present in the Church? Does Scripture offer any solutions? Is there hope for those imprisoned by their cravings? What about those in bondage to their addicted loved ones? Can the Church offer a ministry to the addicted unchurched or to its own members trapped in compulsive lifestyles?

Unfortunately, addictions like alcoholism, drug dependency, child abuse, incest, eating disorders, and workaholism afflict Christians as well as nonChristians. Even more unfortunately, the Church often closes its eyes to this reality. Too often Christians won't admit they struggle with behaviors they can't control.

There are reasons for the denial. Sometimes pride gets in the way. Many Christians can't admit they're gripped by a compulsive dependency. They conceal their addictions and maintain a whitewashed

"Christian" image to protect their "spiritual" reputation, instead of grappling authentically with the dark side of their soul. They may fear losing their "witness to the world," not realizing the world needs to see honest strugglers not pious pretenders. Some churches teach that "Christians don't have those kinds of problems," and to admit an addiction casts doubt on one's salvation. Christians often believe God won't love them if they admit to all that's inside of them, so they simply stop looking there.

Unfortunately, we as Christians can't make the problems of addiction and compulsion go away just by refusing to look at them. The power of God is available to help solve our problems, but only if we acknowledge them honestly. Wrong dependencies keep us in bondage, and Jesus waits to set us free, beginning with our admission that we're enslaved. If believers cannot look at sin—their own and other people's—with honesty, compassion, and a word of hope, who on earth can? The Church must remove its rose-colored glasses and seek to help the addicted—those within as well as those outside its own walls. It's a ministry desperately needed in today's world.

CODEPENDENCY: RELATED TO ADDICTION

But it's not just the addicted who are in bondage and need the Church's help. Those connected to the addict by ties of blood or love are affected as well. In the early days of treatment for addiction (the Alcoholics Anonymous movement, begun in the 1930s), it was assumed that once the alcoholic stopped drinking family life would resume its normal course. But that didn't often happen, and eventually it became apparent that alcoholism was a *family* affair, not just one individual's struggle with a compulsive habit.

Not only did a family suffer from the actions and attitudes of the alcoholic. But also, it was learned that the spouse had developed a recognizable pattern of relating to the alcoholic by continually adjusting to—yet always trying to manage—the alcoholic's behavior, particularly the drinking. Thus, the alcoholic's unhealthy addiction pattern had meshed with the spouse's unhealthy control pattern, and each had fed on and been reinforced by the other.

In addition, the children in that alcoholic home developed their own strategies to adjust to the loss of nurturing from both parents. The roles they played helped the family survive, but in the process the children had to sell out their true selves to maintain the family system. There were more casualties in the war zone of an alcoholic home than was first thought.

With the discovery that the spouse and children played specific and more-or-less predictable roles in supporting the alcoholic in his or her drinking (so that the family would not be destroyed), attention turned toward helping those family members change the negative coping strategies they had learned. The spouse began to be called co-alcoholic, the person whose pattern enabled the alcoholic to continue an alcoholic lifestyle. Later, when the addiction field broadened to include dependencies in addition to alcohol, the term *co-alcoholic* changed to *co-dependent*, designating a person in a close relationship with anyone destructively dependent on any substance or habit.

Thus, the term *codependency* is related to addiction because most codependents are or have been in a relationship with an addicted or compulsive person. In fact, even the addict is codependent in relationships, a fact that becomes obvious once the substance abuse is stopped. But in recent years codependency has been increasingly viewed as an identifiable, unhealthy compulsion in its own right. In other words, a codependent person is "addicted," not to a destructive substance, but to a destructive pattern of relating to other people, a pattern usually learned from childhood in an abusive or nonnurturing home. Codependency *holds a person hostage* to other people's behaviors, moods, or opinions, and the codependent bases his or her worth and actions on someone else's life. It's a terrible bondage.

That explains why, even when an alcoholic or drug abuser got sober or clean, both spouses continued to have relational problems. The destructive patterns of the two partners no longer meshed. Sobriety had been established and the home had become externally less chaotic, but the codependent spouse felt internally more confused and more miserable than ever because the earlier balance, however destructive, had been upset. In addition, the now-sober spouse struggled with similar self-doubts, confusion, and guilt, because the underlying codependency in the addicted person's life had never been addressed either.

Perhaps a working definition of codependency is in order. No clinical description has been agreed upon in the family-systems or addiction-recovery field, but for purposes of this book, we will operate from the following broad definition, which will be examined in greater detail in following chapters:

> *Codependency is a self-focused way of life in which a person blind to his or her true self continually reacts to others being controlled by and seeking to control their behavior, attitudes, and/or opinions, resulting in spiritual sterility, loss of authenticity, and absence of intimacy.*

Codependency is a matter of degree. Everyone feels controlled by people and circumstances at times; codependents feel that way most of their lives. Everyone tries to control others to some extent; codependents think they'll die if they lose control. Everyone has blind spots; codependents live in denial about basic realities in their relationships.

Think of a relationship continuum with healthy mutual interdependence at one end and debilitating codependency at the other. We all fall somewhere in between, but people who live in close relationship to alcoholics, drug abusers, workaholics, or other addicted persons occupy the codependent end of the spectrum.

There are no clear-cut indicators of just when a person steps over the line from being noncodependent to being codependent. With pregnancy, either you are or you aren't; you can't be a little bit pregnant. But a person *can* be a little bit codependent. However, codependency is also progressive, so the longer a person pursues codependent strategies for dealing with life, the more codependent he or she becomes. Eventually those strategies become an addictive way of life—a person's primary and compulsive method for relating to self and others—and we say of that person, "He (or she) is a codependent."

The remainder of this first section (chapters 2-6) will examine several characteristics of the self-focused codependent mentality. The first characteristic we'll consider is *self-forfeiture*, the codependent's loss of self arising from a sense of being controlled by others.

QUESTIONS FOR BUILDING COMMUNITY

1. In a sentence, summarize what you understand addiction to be.
2. How do you understand codependency to be related to alcoholism and other addictions?

3. Give evidence to show that Jenny, the woman described in the opening paragraphs, exhibits the following characteristics of codependency (which will be discussed in coming chapters):
   a. being controlled by others (i.e., victimized),
   b. low sense of self-worth,
   c. trying to control others,
   d. self-sufficiency and isolation,
   e. denial about the family problem.
4. What would be your primary emotion if someone suggested you or someone you love might be addicted to a substance or habit? Why would you feel that way?
5. What would be your primary emotion if someone suggested you or someone you love might be codependent? Why would you feel that way?
6. What would you do if you thought you or someone you love might be addicted or codependent?
7. Why might Christians be more reluctant than unbelievers to acknowledge the presence of an addiction or compulsion in their lives?
8. Should Christians set up addiction or codependency ministries when AA and Al-Anon groups are available in most communities? Why, or why not?

2

SELF-FORFEITURE:
RESIGNED TO HELPLESSNESS

❦

*In order to be intimate, you need a self. Otherwise, getting
close to another person always offers the possibility
of being swallowed up by that person.*
ANNE WILSON SCHAEF
Co-Dependence: Misunderstood, Mistreated

Sitting disconsolate on the edge of her bed trying to make sense of
her life, Jenny thought back to how she had loved Brad—idolized
him, really. He had been everything she'd always dreamed of in a
man—physically strong, sure of himself, fun to be with, a man going
places. He had asked her to go with him, to walk his road and bear his
children. Of course she had said yes. She seemed to have found her very
self in finding Brad.

That, in fact, was part of the problem. Jenny had become so enmeshed
with Brad that she no longer knew who Jenny was. She sometimes wondered if she existed at all. Only Brad seemed real. His successes were
her successes, his failures hers, too. She took his emotional temperature
each morning to determine what her own day would be like. A look or
comment from him could always make or break her mood.

The same was true of Jenny's relationship with the children. When
they were happy, she was happy; their problems felt like her problems.
Last month Jodie took her Scholastic Aptitude Test, and it was Jenny
who felt nervous and uptight. She had lived her life for—and perhaps
through—her daughters, anticipating their needs and meeting them in
spite of any inconvenience. She had cooked for, done homework with,

comforted, cleaned up after, instructed, shopped for, attended the athletic events of, and chauffeured them for over eighteen years. In fact, she couldn't remember what it was like to do something just for herself. If asked, she would have said doing things for herself felt selfish.

Jenny wasn't the person she'd been when she married Brad. In fact, she wasn't sure what sort of person she was at all. She was beginning to realize that who she was depended too much on whom she was with at any given moment. Chameleonlike, she had become expert at being (and doing) whatever was expected, unable to determine for sure what she was like or what she liked.

Jenny had the keen sense she was running out of options. She felt trapped, without choice, compelled to live as she had always lived with Brad. Her absence of choice evidenced itself particularly in two areas: feeling controlled (especially by Brad) and forfeiting her true self. Let's examine both areas in greater detail, because they characterize the experience of most codependents.

CONTROL BY OTHERS

The first aspect of feeling powerless in relationships is the sense of *having one's life controlled by someone else.* Usually a codependent can point to someone (a relative or close friend) whose behavior, attitudes, or opinions "make" them do things they don't really want to do. Codependents say things like, "I always have to organize my schedule around my children's plans," or "My husband made me lie to his boss because he had a hangover again," or "I have to bake a casserole for my sick friend."

As I look back over my own history of codependency and consider the times I have felt most choiceless, one incident in particular comes to mind.

At that time, Bill and I had been married less than five years, and we were living with our three-year-old son, Christopher, in the Florida Keys. Bill was a park ranger at Bahia Honda State Park, and our home was a trailer in a small complex that housed the ranger families across from the main park. It was not uncommon for the rangers and their families to party together in our communal yard on the weekends. The partying inevitably included considerable drinking, which made me particularly uncomfortable because I'd grown up in an alcoholic home and was repulsed by any kind of drunkenness.

On this particular Saturday night the party ran longer than usual, and Bill's drinking had made him uncharacteristically belligerent. Appalled when his intended fistfight with another ranger at our doorstep had to be halted by the propitious intervention of friends, I heaved a huge sigh of relief soon afterward when he fell into bed, oblivious to everything, including my inner terror and chaos.

Until then I had pushed my anxiety about Bill's drinking to the back of my mind, but that night was different. My horror of conflict and fear that I'd married an alcoholic forced itself into my unwilling awareness, and I was terrified. Feeling utterly out of control, I walked out into the moonlight past our now-quiet neighborhood and came to a large flat rock where I sat and cried out in helplessness to God. "What am I going to do? What will become of Christopher and me? God, why did You allow me to get into a mess like this?"

My helplessness that night ought to have thrust me, not only into dependence on God, but also into a willingness to face the underlying dynamics of my own codependency and to change my destructive pattern of protecting Bill from the consequences of his drinking. Unfortunately, that did not happen until things were much worse for Bill and me. But I remember how victimized I felt back then, and how compulsively I went back the next day both into denial and into trying to control Bill's drinking. Because getting well wasn't an option for me then, I had to keep running from reality, which kept me feeling crazy and out of control for years.

Compulsive behaviors make the person who engages in them feel helpless to do things differently. Robbed of options by the real or imagined reactions of others, codependents like Jenny and me live at the mercy of others' demands or expectations, and we end up feeling *used* and *powerless*. We look to others for permission to do something or be someone, and the loss of empowerment results in a profound anger or depression we can neither change nor understand. Without choice, codependents feel driven, helpless, victimized.

VICTIMIZATION

The particulars of victimization may vary from individual to individual, but the pattern is remarkably similar. Someone indicates a need by a word, a glance, or a mood, and the codependent immediately knows what must be done: Meet that need, no matter what the personal cost in terms of time, energy, even principle. In the mind of the codependent, the other person's request or insinuation always takes precedence over his or her own plans, feelings, or personal agenda. Time and time again the decision is made: *Do what the other person wants done.* And time and time again the resentment builds: Why do I always get stuck with the dirty end of every deal? The victim mentality is thus reinforced, and the sense of powerlessness increases.

It is a vicious cycle, and just telling the codependent to stop doing it is not enough. The victimization, like the codependency itself, has taken on a life of its own. Being a victim is a compulsion the codependent is unable to just stop. It will take an entirely new way of looking at oneself, of looking at and living life, for a person like Jenny to change her victimized pattern of dealing with her family. It will take the very power of God. In a later chapter we will examine in more detail what is needed for changing an established pattern of self-victimization.

KING WITHOUT A SELF

King Ahab, whose story is found in 1 Kings 21, is an example of a man who felt powerless to manage his life. Naboth, one of Ahab's subjects, owned a vineyard adjacent to the palace that Ahab wanted, even though he knew God had forbidden such a sale of one's real estate inheritance. When Naboth refused to sell his vineyard to the king, "Ahab went home, sullen and angry. . . . He lay on his bed sulking and refused to eat" (verse 4).

Ahab was thwarted; he couldn't get what he felt he needed to make him happy, so he played the role of martyr, hoping someone would take up his cause. His wife, Jezebel, was glad to comply: "'Get up and eat! Cheer up. I'll get you the vineyard of Naboth the Jezreelite,'" she told him (verse 7).

Ahab knew Jezebel would have to resort to treachery to accomplish *his* goal, yet he yielded his power to her. He lacked the inner substance either to stand up to her (by forbidding her interference) or to do himself what he knew was right (by accepting with grace Naboth's godly decision). Ahab's personal abdication, however, didn't negate his accountability before God. Jezebel's successful conspiracy to have

Naboth murdered was considered to be Ahab's sin in God's eyes; both its punishment and its later postponement because of Ahab's repentance were the result of Ahab's responsibility for his chosen abdication to his wife's control (verses 19-24).

The chronicler added this comment: "There was never a man like Ahab, who sold himself to do evil in the eyes of the LORD, urged on by Jezebel his wife" (verse 25). Ahab's self-forfeiture was ultimately his own choice, and it had dire consequences for himself, his family, and all Israel.

EXTERNAL REFERENTING

Feeling powerless in relationships isn't just about feeling controlled by others; it's also about feeling like a nonperson. Many codependents sense they exist only as an extension of someone else. They don't know their own thoughts, opinions, or preferences, because over the years they've become too involved in sensing and reacting to other people's thoughts, opinions, and preferences. One of the earliest clues I had that I was codependent was when someone asked me what my favorite color was and I realized I had no idea. I felt like the friend of mine who once turned to her companion in a clothing store and asked, "Do I like this shirt?"

Psychologists call this tendency to adopt the opinions or moods of others *external referenting*. External referenting means a person takes his or her cues about what to think and believe, or how to talk and behave, from other people. Codependents use someone or something outside themselves as a reference point for who they should be or what they should do. Jenny, for example, would be having a good day until Brad came home in a terrible mood, and then she ended up having a bad day, too. A recovering codependent I know said it was "hard work" to retain his own healthy emotional outlook when he was with his family, instead of giving in to their negative and destructive way of seeing life. Finding and being oneself are not easy.

BLURRING OF BOUNDARIES

Another common codependent phenonemon closely related to external referenting is the blurring of boundaries. People with blurred boundaries don't know where they end and where the other person begins in a relationship. They are enmeshed, unable to separate the feelings or experiences of one from the other. There was a time when I wasn't sure whether it was I or my husband who had experienced physical abuse in childhood; Bill's history had become fused with my own. Someone once said, "You know you're codependent when you're drowning and someone else's life flashes before your eyes."

Codependents with blurred boundaries often allow someone else to hurt or abuse them because they somehow think that person has a right to invade their privacy, plans, or personal well-being with impunity. Sexually abused children, for example, believe they have no boundaries, that the doorknob is always on the outside of their door and they are on the inside with no right to set limits. Who they really are becomes lost in the avalanche of other people's intentions and definitions of who they are. Jenny said nothing if Brad verbally abused her with critical and destructive words when he was drinking, nor did she intervene for her children when Brad did the same to them. Because she wasn't sure of who she was or what her limits ought to be, she thought Brad had the right to mistreat her as he might mistreat himself. In fact, some messages she heard in church regarding submission reinforced her belief that she didn't have *any* rights to claim for herself in relationship to Brad. Jenny's perceived absence of choice with regard to Brad was related to her absence of boundaries with regard to herself.

Codependents deeply enmeshed with another person often fail to take basic care of themselves. They don't pay attention to their own needs or feelings because they don't think their needs or feelings have any validity. Though Jenny was angry with Brad, she didn't really believe her anger was legitimate. Accustomed to living in Brad's skin and seeing things from his point of view, she couldn't admit his drinking was alcoholic, because *he* didn't see it as alcoholic. Unable to own her own fear, anger, and despair, Jenny felt she was going crazy. She'd lost herself and had no idea how to find what she had lost.

WAS JESUS CONTROLLED BY OTHERS?

One of the confusing things about codependency is that codependent behaviors often masquerade as Christian virtues. Jesus instructed us to love others as ourselves, to offer the other cheek to those who strike us.

The Apostle Paul said we are to consider others better than ourselves and to bear one another's burdens. Losing one's self and sacrificing for others seem to be the biblical epitome of piety. Is codependency the scriptural norm? Should believers seek to become glad victims of other people's mistreatment?

Let's look at Jesus. Was He codependent? Did He let Himself be controlled by others, a victim without choices?

Jesus' life reveals that He never let people control His decisions, neither by their mood, expectations, or behavior. Far from being a victim, He willingly chose to serve others, but not because He had to. When He washed the disciples' feet on the day before His death, the Apostle John revealed the internal context of Jesus' decision:

> Jesus knew that the Father had put all things under his power, and that he had come from God and was returning to God; so he got up from the meal, took off his outer clothing, and wrapped a towel around his waist. After that, he poured water into a basin and began to wash his disciples' feet, drying them with the towel that was wrapped around him. (John 13:3-5)

Jesus didn't feel pressured to wash the dirty feet of His tired and hungry disciples so they would like Him. He didn't feel they were controlling Him and He had no other choice. Rather, Jesus was aware of His position, *freely choosing* this task because He "knew that the Father had put all things under his power."

Far from being a victim, Jesus even consented to the place, time, and manner of His own dying (Matthew 16:21, John 12:31-33). He said, "The reason my Father loves me is that I lay down my life—only to take it up again. No one takes it from me, but I lay it down of my own accord" (John 10:17-18). He surely was troubled in Gethsemane as He faced His coming crucifixion, but His words were not the words of a helpless victim. He *chose* to die.

WAS JESUS A NONPERSON?

Did Jesus forfeit Himself or sacrifice His personhood when He chose servanthood? Was He externally referenced, taking His identity from what others thought or expected of Him? Were His boundaries blurred so that He allowed His detractors to oppose His ministry without interference?

In contrast to the frail identities many codependents have, Jesus always knew clearly who He was and what His purposes were. He knew He had come from Heaven to do the will of His Father (John 6:38), and His identity never gave way to the expectations of others. He didn't let the crowd crown Him (John 6:15), though He realized He deserved and would one day receive their homage. He acknowledged as true His good friend Peter's declaration that He was Messiah (Matthew 16:16-17), but He soon afterward rebuked him for insisting He need not die as the messianic sacrifice (16:21-23). Jesus never allowed Himself to be squeezed into anyone's mold, no matter how friendly or antagonistic the push. When the Pharisees opposed His ministry, He minced no words, publicly rebuking them for their disbelief, even though they represented the most respected party of the religious establishment of His day (Matthew 23). Though Jesus gave unstintingly of Himself in genuine love during His entire life, it cannot be said that He ever lost or gave up His sense of self.

SUMMING UP

The marriage of Jenny and Brad is one example of the kind of relationship in which millions of people find themselves trapped. Codependents feel controlled by others and have lost a sense of their own personhood. Unsure of who they are and feeling powerless to manage their lives, codependents—even Christians trapped in codependency—cannot live authentically. Their behaviors might mimic the way Jesus lived, but in their inner spirits they are far from being the free, loving, glad servants Jesus modeled to His disciples. In fact, they see themselves as not only powerless but essentially worthless. In the next chapter we'll take a look at an altogether different type of codependent and consider how codependents view themselves.

QUESTIONS FOR BUILDING COMMUNITY

1. From the case study of Jenny and Brad, give specific examples of how Jenny felt
   a. powerless (controlled by others), and

b. enmeshed (overly identified with other people and their feelings).

2. What is the difference between enmeshment and empathy?
3. In your own words tell what is meant by the codependent character-istic of "self-forfeiture."
4. Do you see any evidence of self-forfeiture in yourself or someone you love? Explain.
5. Name a specific circumstance (one not mentioned in this chapter) in which Jesus might have appeared to be a victim; then explain why He was *not* a victim in that circumstance.
6. Codependents often evidence "Christian" behaviors, like sacrificing their own preferences or convenience for the sake of others. Give an example of how a seemingly unselfish behavior might actually be a codependent behavior.
7. Why would our spiritual enemy (Satan) *not* want Christians to acknowledge their addictions or codependency?

3

SELF-CONTEMPT:
INCLINED TO FEEL WORTHLESS

❦

People get into this place of perceived powerlessness.
They believe that they are bad and unworthy and there
is nothing they can do to change. People stay in painful
circumstances, jobs and relationships because they feel
they do not deserve anything any better.
SHARON WEGSCHEIDER-CRUSE
The Miracle of Recovery

Andrea is a social worker responsible for supervising neglected and abused children who come under the protection and jurisdiction of the state. Competent and caring, Andrea is respected by her superiors and by the judges and lawyers with whom she works. Having herself been raised in an abusive home where she took responsibility for the emotional well-being of the family from about age ten, Andrea takes pride in her ability to help these damaged children, primarily adolescents. Her caseload is heavy to the point of exhaustion, but Andrea never complains; it is another point of pride with her that she can handle the stress of her job.

Because she understands and works intimately with disturbed children, Andrea tends to draw her friendships at work and church from people who were themselves abused or neglected in childhood. She feels comfortable in the role of helper and avoids relationships with those who aren't needy. Of course, her needy friends end up using her, and Andrea sometimes resents the drain on her time and energy. She seldom enjoys any reciprocity of friendship. But her resentment and loneliness are well-kept secrets—even from herself. Andrea would be shocked to realize self-contempt and rage beneath her "helper" facade.

People in Andrea's church see her as strong, "together," and a good listener. Yet no one would describe her as vulnerable or approachable on an intimate level. She never leans on her friends, never outwardly asks anything of anyone. She wouldn't say so, but her deep belief is that she doesn't deserve to be helped, but only to give help.

Yet Andrea holds the unspoken expectation that those she helps should feel grateful, admiring, and somehow in awe of her. A friend who eventually becomes strong enough to not "need" Andrea anymore usually ends up losing her friendship because the rules and roles have changed. Unable to risk not being in charge, Andrea keeps her relationships one step removed from genuine involvement, except at the level of offering her expertise as counselor. To be needy herself would be not only uncomfortable but also repulsive and even terrifying. It's much safer for her to remain in charge.

If Andrea would risk an honest look inside herself, she would see her many codependent characteristics: her loss of authenticity (she *must* play the role of helper); her compulsive need for approval (through others' validation of her counseling skills); and her unwitting self-contempt (her belief that she has nothing to offer *except* her expertise). Andrea protectively distances herself from others because *she fears being exposed as the nobody she unconsciously thinks she is.* Despising the lonely, needy woman within, Andrea clings desperately to the competent image she presents to the world.

Codependents don't all look alike. Andrea isn't married to an alcoholic or abuser as Jenny is, but both are codependent. Both are essentially adjusters, people damaged by childhood experiences who cope with their world by trying to please and who end up being controlled instead—Jenny by her bondage to her family, Andrea by her bondage to playing the counselor role in all her relationships. Andrea is no more authentic in her relationships than Jenny is. Both are desperate for the approval of others, and both inwardly despise their inner selves, unable to simply be who they are in their relationships. And though neither is aware of it, both are deeply committed to living life on their own terms, not God's.

APPROVAL JUNKIES

An important part of the bondage called codependency is the compulsive need to be approved by others. This need, often unconscious, runs deep and controls virtually every decision the codependent makes. Loss of approval feels like death. It is a terrible addiction.

Approval junkies live as hostages to other people's opinions and judgments regarding their thoughts, motives, feelings, or behaviors. Approval seekers look good; they have to. Sometimes the most ardent people-pleasers are elected as church leaders and seem to be the most successful Christians around, fooling themselves into thinking they're trying to please so people will be drawn to Jesus.

But people-pleasing isn't godly, nor is it healthy. Appeasers usually end up feeling used, unappreciated, and driven to become all things to all people in order to maintain their image and receive continued approval. They appear giving, but in fact they are enslaved to their insatiable need to be admired.

The approval junkie mentality isn't just about marital or romantic relationships. My own codependency, though most visible and deeply rooted in my relationship with Bill, also exists in virtually every relationship I have—with my parents, my child, my siblings, my editors, my friends and neighbors. Even the grocery store clerk and the man who delivers our bottled water are involved in my codependency. My need to be approved is generic; I want everyone who touches my life to affirm me. Other codependents may not play so wide a field, but the compulsion surely is not limited to marriage or romance. Codependency can afflict anyone in relationship with someone he or she cares about and wishes to favorably impress.

The codependent's need for others' affirmation often controls his or her decisions, actions, attitude, or mood. Jenny was too desperate for Brad's approval to confront the destructive influence his drinking was having on her and the entire family. Andrea built her life around proving herself so competent that her boss and clients and friends would say only admiring things about her. Terrified of others' disapproval, both felt they would die or *cease to exist* as persons if others didn't affirm them. Though Jenny's appeasing didn't guarantee Brad's affirmation (she couldn't always predict his mood or expectations) and Andrea's "expertise" eventually lost her the close friendships she deeply desired, both codependents nevertheless compulsively sought approval despite the personal cost to themselves. Groveling for affirmation, they were willing to accept mere crumbs even in their most important relationships. At the core of their beings, they felt like zeros and were unknowingly enraged that they weren't receiving what they couldn't even recognize they wanted.

A KING DESPERATE TO PLEASE

King Saul at one level could be considered an approval junkie, small in his own eyes (1 Samuel 15:17) and painfully conscious of his inadequacies (1 Samuel 9:21). When his coronation moment arrived, he had to be brought out of his hiding place among the baggage (1 Samuel 10:22). What may appear at first to be godly humility, however, eventually showed itself to be a desperate fear of shame and a fierce commitment to personal autonomy. The difference is crucial.

People-pleasers lack the strength of character necessary to confront what may be a wrong attitude or action on the part of themselves or someone else. Soon after the beginning of Saul's reign, for example, he mustered his troops at Gilgal to fight the Philistines, and his men became increasingly fearful to the point of desertion while waiting for Samuel the priest to come and offer the required sacrifice. Rather than encourage his men by his own example of patient strength and faith in God, Saul yielded to his soldiers' pressure and offered the sacrifice himself, clearly a violation of God's command. He said he had no choice, trying to justify his deliberate disobedience by telling Samuel, "I felt compelled to offer the burnt offering" (1 Samuel 13:12). It was the beginning of the end for Saul's dynasty.

Saul's compulsion to please others instead of following hard after God, to look good to his people no matter what, is most clearly seen in his rebellion against God's instruction to destroy utterly the Amalekites and all their possessions. Saul conspired with his men to save the Amalekite king and the best of the animals for sacrifices, explaining to Samuel, "I was afraid of the people and so I gave in to them" (verse 24).But Samuel named Saul's deepest problem, not people-pleasing nor insecurity, but rebellion and arrogance against God. Samuel compared it to "the sin of divination" and "the evil of idolatry" and announced God's judgment against Saul: "Because you have rejected the word of the LORD, he has rejected you as king" (1 Samuel 15:23). Even in the face of this judgment Saul refused to genuinely repent, revealing the real intent of his heart when he begged Samuel, "I have sinned. But please honor me before the elders of my people and before Israel" (verse 30). Saul's sorrow was not for his disobedience but for his loss of prestige before the people. For approval junkies, it is not rebellion against God that feels like death, but looking bad.

LIES CODEPENDENTS BELIEVE

King Saul's desperate hunger for the approval of others, because he was small in his own eyes, had its roots in a stubborn spirit of independence from God. His failure to repent of his arrogance shows the depth of his commitment to Satan's lie about where a person's worth should come from. In his book on self-esteem, *The Search for Significance*, Robert McGee discussed several lies Satan uses to keep people from experiencing an appropriate self-worth. One lie regarding the insatiable need for approval is, *"I must be approved (accepted) by certain others to feel good about myself."*[1] In other words, I can't have a good self-image unless certain people approve of my attitudes, actions, moods, or personhood. Codependents are approval-seekers, making themselves, like Saul, hostages to their chosen emotional kidnappers, even as they remain unaware of the deeper issues at stake in their souls..

The acceptance must come from the parent(s), spouse, friend, child, or group the codependent has in mind; anyone else's approval won't satisfy. The approval-giver doesn't have to live with or near the codependent. The person doesn't even have to be alive. Many codependents live their entire lives trying to please a long-deceased mother or father who never approved of them while alive. Often a particular sentence or judgment passed by the parent during a moment of anger, drunkenness, or frustration ("You're nothing but a slut!" or "You'll never amount to anything!") will live in the memory of the child long into adulthood. Sometimes the words are not consciously remembered, but the codependent will be driven to prove that he or she is *not* lazy, ugly, dirty, incompetent, stupid, or a failure, as those parental words spoken long ago labeled him or her. Approval from beyond the grave is never achievable, but that doesn't lessen the compulsive efforts many codependents expend to earn it anyway.

Approval junkies live with an inordinate fear of rejection. No one likes rejection, but the codependent believes rejection equals death— death to the self, death to any possibility of believing oneself worthwhile. The rejection need not be loud or public; it need not be spoken at all. A word, a glance, a silence, an absence of affirmation—all can effectively kill or maim. Often the one withholding the approval is aware of his or her power to control or punish the one hungry for affirmation, and the dance of manipulation played out between them can be poignantly pathetic. I know. I have seen the dance swirl. I have danced it myself.

WORTHLESS

Though codependents often find themselves in bondage to their desperate fear of rejection, they seldom experience the deep level of approval they crave. In fact, they often receive criticism, demeaning, or disapproval from others. Consequently, perhaps their most common characteristic is a low sense of self-worth. Virtually every book written on the subject of codependency includes a section on poor self-esteem.

An essential aspect of self-esteem is our own inner perception of whether or not we're worthwhile. Codependents often grew up in homes where children and their needs were considered less worthy than something else—alcohol, drugs, sexual satisfaction, the neighbors' (or deacons') opinion, convenience, making money, keeping peace in the family, time with friends, and so on. When children are consistently given a low priority, they bring into adult life a belief that they are unworthy of love and esteem, especially if they have failed to measure up to the performance expected of them.

The conspiracy against self-valuing is abetted by the notion implicitly (and sometimes explicitly) taught by our contemporary culture that only the rich, bright, good-looking, productive, unfailingly successful, and popular people are worthwhile. Those who don't measure up to the ideal should be ignored, punished, or ostracized. As Robert McGee wrote, a lie Satan wants us to believe is, *"Those who fail are unworthy of love and deserve to be punished."*[2] Codependents who sense they are not worth much also believe they deserve whatever bad (i.e., nonnurturing, even abusive) treatment other people hand out. They have it coming because they failed to do what they should have done (or did what they shouldn't have done). Mistreatment fits into their pyschological scheme of things and feels appropriate (though painful). The expectation of emotional deprivation goes hand in hand with low self-esteem.

Thus, even though Jenny desperately wanted to relieve the pain and emotional chaos Brad's drinking was bringing, a part of her felt she didn't really deserve a happy home or kind treatment from her husband and children. After all, she hadn't always been the perfectly loving wife and mother she had wanted and always tried to be. And Andrea viewed herself as worthwhile only as a counselor. Though she took pride in that role, she also felt empty inside and undeserving of anything deeper. Both codependents believed the lie: *Those who fail are unworthy of love.* They didn't deserve to be happy; they should have tried harder.

SELF-CONTEMPT

People with low self-esteem participate with their detractors through self-destructive behaviors consistent with their own deep sense of inferiority. Codependents feel trapped by past failures and doomed to repeat those failures in the future. Their self-contempt can be verbal or behavioral, announcing to the world: "I don't deserve anything good because I'm worthless. I don't blame you for not liking me; I don't like me, either."

Self-contempt can wear many faces, sometimes passing for humility or selflessness. Sally grew up in a poor family in which both parents worked and she had the care of her two younger brothers. She managed well, and her parents praised but never nurtured her. Unaware that the nurturing loss left her feeling unlovable, Sally, now a middle-aged widow, meets her unmet intimacy needs by caring for all thirteen shut-ins in her church. When someone compliments her, she says, "Oh, I could have done more. Maybe God will bless my efforts in spite of me." Her words sound modest, but in fact they come from Sally's low opinion of herself—which she secretly hopes will be contradicted by the person praising her.

Angie, a young mother, was sexually abused for years by her father, a respected deacon in the church. Her husband, Jake, batters her emotionally with critical, demeaning words. Because Angie blames and despises herself for the childhood incest, she never defends herself. She thinks she deserves Jake's accusations and keeps trying harder to be the loving, chaste wife she inwardly despairs of ever being. Pregnant with their second child, Angie prays for another boy. If Jake were to abuse a daughter, Angie is terrified of what she might do.

Charlie is a good-looking man in his early thirties, established in a well-paying job and actively involved in his local church. His mother died when he was ten, and no one helped him deal with his anger and abandonment over her death. Charlie unconsciously believes the death was his fault and he doesn't deserve to be loved. Now an adult, Charlie can't seem to find the "right" woman. He keeps stumbling into and out of stormy relationships with troubled women, not realizing his choices serve to confirm his own low estimate of himself. Charlie doesn't know it, but his self-contempt is showing.

These are some of the ways self-contempt reveals itself. Often it is internal—the negative sentences we say to ourselves about ourselves in our quiet moments. But however self-contempt is lived out, it is an expression of the belief that one's personhood is *hopelessly flawed* and unchangeable. Whether by word, action, or inaction, those who hold themselves in contempt pursue habitually destructive patterns that keep them bound to their own low view of their worth.

SELF-NEGLECT

What follows self-contempt, both logically and chronologically, is self-neglect. Self-neglect may be mild, like feeling guilty for spending time or money on oneself. Or it may be more severe, like the woman who refuses to see her doctor about a cancerous growth on her neck because she doesn't believe she's worth the money it would take to deal with the problem. Some codependents allow themselves to be repeatedly abused because they hate themselves. If followed to its logical conclusion, self-neglect can lead to attempts at suicide, or perhaps the more subtle "slow suicide" of disorders, such as anorexia, drug addiction, or alcohol abuse. Self-contempt is more than just a poor choice of attitude; it can endanger one's very life.

JESUS AND SELF-CONTEMPT

When Jesus walked this earth, He modeled how we ought to view ourselves. Nowhere in Scripture do we find Him devaluing Himself. Though He came to sacrifice His very life for His beloved, He never minimized His worth. On the contrary, He referred often to His value to the Father, particularly in His private teaching times with His disciples (see John 14–17). Jesus never spoke negative words about His work or His person.

As an extension of that self-awareness of His own worth, Jesus seemed to know the value of self-care. He regularly scheduled time alone with His Father, away from the demands of the crowd, and planned time to be just with His disciples. Jesus made no apology for attending weddings and dinner parties with His close friends; He knew He needed the refreshment of spirit that came from such relaxation.

Jesus was confidently aware of His own value. Self-contempt was the farthest thing from His mind. He enjoyed equality with the God of the universe (Philippians 2:6-7), and in that awareness He yielded His rights for the sake of His chosen. The two go together: self-valuing and genuine love. Jesus' intimate relationship of total dependence on His Father enabled Him to deal both confidently and lovingly with everyone with whom He came in contact.

One of the diabolical things about codependency is that it insists on being self-preoccupied. There is a personal payoff for codependents who relinquish their sense of self and worth. Simply stated, *it's easy for codependents to justify relational irresponsibility if there's "no one home" in their souls.* Focusing on victimization brings release from the obligation of choosing to love wisely and well.

The codependent's unspoken argument runs like this: "I've been victimized, so don't ask me to risk being hurt again by reaching out to anyone." Or, "I'm nobody, and you would never expect a nobody to come through on your behalf." Thus codependents justify their love failures by hiding behind their victimization and loss of self.

As awful as being victimized (and revictimized) is, in a perverse way it is "safer" than being held accountable for taking charge of one's own life and making difficult choices to love well. It is terrible to feel worthless, but there's a certain relief at not being required to offer one's soul to bless another person's life. Suffering the loss of choice and self-esteem is often the codependent's ticket to irresponsible living. Whether consciously or not, the codependent declares, "Don't ask much of me; I've been wounded before, and I don't intend to be wounded again."

SUMMING UP

The denigration of self as experienced and lived out by codependents finds no basis in Scripture, particularly not in the life of Jesus. The Bible never supports the "approval junkie" mentality as godly, let alone mentally healthy. What fuels a codependent's low self-esteem and feverish approval-seeking is not faith but fear—fear of failure, fear of abandonment, fear of rejection, fear of loving others responsibly, and fear of "punishment" from those whose approval signals life and whose disapproval threatens personal death. Codependents do not like themselves, do not take care of themselves, and often participate in their own victimization. Contrary to the message of Scripture and to the example of Jesus, people caught in a codependent lifestyle act out their deep sense of shame and inferiority through self-contemptuous and even self-destructive words, attitudes, and behaviors. It's no fun living with someone who doesn't like you, especially when that someone is you.

The next chapter will examine the ways codependents deal with their low self-valuing through their attempts to control their world.

QUESTIONS FOR BUILDING COMMUNITY

1. Show how Andrea evidences one or more of the following codependent characteristics:
    a. being controlled by others,
    b. low sense of self-worth,
    c. trying to control others,
    d. self-sufficiency and isolation,
    e. denial about her problem.
2. Explain the difference between self-contempt and humility.
3. Explain how your own childhood relationship with your parents has helped you to have a negative or positive view of yourself.
4. How is it possible for someone (especially a parent) to control a person even from beyond the grave? Give an example.
5. Everyone prefers acceptance to rejection. What sets a codependent apart from a more "normal" person in this regard?
6. Why does living with a person addicted to a substance or a destructive behavior almost always result in the codependent developing low self-esteem?
7. How can self-contempt (i.e., low self-esteem) be dangerous?
8. How might low self-esteem be a perverse "advantage" to a codependent? Give a specific example from your life or someone else's.

NOTES
1. Robert S. McGee, *The Search for Significance* (Houston, TX: Rapha Publishing, 1987), page 30.
2. McGee, page 68.

4

SELF-AGGRANDIZEMENT: DESPERATE TO CONTROL

❦

One must be in control of all interactions,
feelings and personal behavior at all times.
This is the cardinal rule
of all dysfunctional shame-based family systems.
JOHN BRADSHAW
Bradshaw On: The Family

Lois is married to Joe, a full-fledged workaholic—conscientious, hard-driving, successful—and a committed Christian deeply involved in his church. Their friends think they have the ideal marriage. So did they, until they moved to a new city and Lois began to feel the loss of her friends, her part-time job, and her role as facilitator in her church's evangelism training program. Joe's obsession with his work, which had intensified in an effort to "prove himself" to a new boss in a new setting, left her feeling a keen loneliness.

It wasn't just that Lois needed to find a new niche for herself. For the first time in their marriage she realized she needed Joe deeply—his involvement in her life, his help with their teenage sons—and Joe wasn't available. She resented his drivenness to put in hours of uncompensated work—time that should have been devoted to his family.

What especially concerned Lois was that sixteen-year-old Allen, their older son, was getting in trouble at his new school because of his involvement with friends known to be drug users. At Lois's request, Joe confronted him. Allen denied he'd ever experimented with drugs, but Lois was sure he was lying. Joe, on the other hand, was glad to believe Allen because it meant Joe could continue his undivided attention to his new job and his duties in their new church.

Lois was now the "heavy" with both husband and son. Needing Joe's support for herself and for Allen, she increased her complaints and demands that her husband spend more time meeting the family's emotional needs. She also tightened her surveillance of Allen's friends and activities, lecturing him repeatedly about the dangers of drug use and nagging him when he skipped school or violated his curfew.

As the situation at home worsened toward chaos, Lois intensified her efforts to change her husband and her son. She was afraid to share her fears with her untried Christian friends; her reputation as a wife, mother, and church leader was at stake. Haunted by the specter of Allen's slide into addiction and Joe's preoccupied indifference, Lois tried desperately to control her world. And in her panic to avert disaster, Lois failed to realize that Kenny, their compliant twelve-year-old, was being lost in the shuffle just as he was about to embark on his own journey into adolescence.

THE NEED TO CONTROL

One of the most significant issues a codependent faces is the issue of control. In chapter 2 we considered the choicelessness codependents experience, the sense of being controlled or victimized by others. Yet, strange as it seems, codependents also try desperately to control the actions or moods of those they love. They're determined to ensure the "good" behavior of their spouse, parent, child, or friend ("good" being defined as sober, straight, law-abiding, nonviolent, involved—whatever is the opposite of the loved one's usual destructive behavior). All efforts to control people or circumstances reflect the strong desire codependents have for self-aggrandizement—for making themselves feel or appear more powerful than they really are in the face of the deep sense of powerlessness they actually experience.

During my growing-up years, I took responsibility for maintaining the emotional well-being of everyone in my family, including my parents. No one assigned me the role; I just took it on. But in order to pull it off, I had to control what happened—tuning in on every family conversation, anticipating problems, planning out solutions, and always being available to make things right—without seeming pushy, of course. Little wonder I had colitis from junior high on.

A codependent's control takes many forms, all of which violate both the *dignity of responsibility* and the *freedom of choice* God intended us to offer and enjoy. Two control strategies in particular stand out: *rescuing* and *caretaking*.

RESCUING: REMOVING THE DIGNITY OF RESPONSIBILITY

Rescuing is what a person does to save others from the negative consequences of their choices. Parents who won't hold a child responsible to pay for what he broke or lost are pulling off an illegitimate rescue. A husband who lies to his drug-addicted wife's boss or to his family about his wife's true physical condition is refusing her the dignity of responsibility.

Sometimes codependents rescue by doing something they should not do. When Jenny went downtown to bring Brad home from his drinking binge, she was rescuing. Sometimes a rescue involves failing to do what we ought to do. Joe and Lois by their indifference and inaction are unwittingly rescuing Allen from the consequences of his choices to skip school and hang out with undesirable friends. Sometimes a rescue includes both wrong action and irresponsible inaction. My son knows how to load the dishwasher the right way, but to avoid a conflict, I'll redo his shabby job instead of disciplining him for not doing it right. Rescuing intends to save the pride, comfort, reputation, job, or finances of the "rescuee." Codependents feel they owe it to the ones they love.

ELI THE ENABLER

Eli, God's high priest during the Israelite period of the judges, was committed to rescuing his sons, Hophni and Phinehas, from the consequences of their sinful choices. Scripture declares succinctly, "Eli's sons were wicked men" (1 Samuel 2:12). They demanded for themselves the best portions of the sacrificial animals and slept with the women who served at the tabernacle (2:17,22). Eli knew about his sons' wickedness, but instead of taking action, he tried to control them with a warning (2:22-25).

God confronted Eli's sin: "Why do you honor your sons more than me by fattening yourselves on the choice parts of every offering made by my people Israel?" (2:29). Later He said to Samuel, "I told [Eli] that I would judge his family forever because of the sin he knew about; his sons made themselves contemptible, and he failed to restrain them. Therefore, I swore to the house of Eli, 'The guilt of Eli's house will never be atoned for by sacrifice or offering'" (3:13-14).

Eli had tried to control Hophni and Phinehas with words, but his attempt was both demeaning and ineffectual. If Eli had restrained his sons by removing them from their priestly office, it would have shown he was giving up trying to control their behavior and was simply allowing the just consequences of his sons' wickedness to fall. Eli's "protection" of Hophni and Phinehas rescued them from immediate pain but eventually brought disaster on his own family and on the entire house of Israel.

RESCUING AS A FAILURE TO LOVE

A codependent's controlling doesn't show the recipient any kindness. Rescuing feels heroic to the rescuer, but it robs the "rescuee" of the self-respect that comes from knowing his or her choices matter (and therefore the "rescuee" matters) because his or her choosing has consequences. A rescuer gives this message: "You can be foolish if you want because I'll be the strong one to save you from yourself." By allowing himself or herself to be rescued, the workaholic or alcoholic or rebellious child ends up feeling incompetent, managed, and babied—to say nothing of the damage caused by the long-term consequences of his or her irresponsibility. Eli might have been able to save his sons from death and the nation from judgment had he been willing to confront rather than accommodate his sons' wickedness. Rescuing looks loving, but in fact it results in disrespect and deep resentment on both sides: The one being rescued resents the attempted control, and the codependent resents the ineffectiveness of and ingratitude for the rescuing.

It won't work to tell the codependent, "Stop rescuing your addicted spouse or delinquent child." There is something compulsive about the role, as though the codependent's identity resides in being the "savior," the one in charge of the situation. This hidden payback of real or imagined control, which is integral to the savior role, actually feels quite good to the codependent. It feels powerful and noble. Dr. Dan Allender describes this savior mentality (or false martyrdom) as using others as the high ground for our own crucifixion.[1] People see the codependent as the poor suffering martyr, the only "good guy" in the family, casting everyone else into the villain role. It is a pernicious form of codependent control.

CARETAKING: DENYING THE FREEDOM OF CHOICE

Another common control mechanism is caretaking: the acts a person does for others that they could and should do for themselves. I have a codependent friend who feels compelled to warn her doctor about overcommitting his time with her, so he won't neglect his other patients—a responsibility he can certainly handle himself. Jenny and Lois likewise shield their family and friends from any irritation or problem that might upset those loved ones and bring anger or disapproval back on Jenny and Lois.

Caretaking is not to be confused with caregiving. Caregiving is what a person freely does for others that they cannot or need not do for themselves. The unselfishness of people who lovingly minister to disabled or discouraged friends, children, or parents bears no resemblance to codependent caretaking.

A caretaker operates on the assumption that his or her way is the only right way. Moreover, the person at the receiving end of the codependent's caretaking is assumed to be incompetent to accomplish the task at hand successfully. There is the woman who tells her husband which traffic lane to drive in or what the speed limit is. And then there's the father who gets up from a sickbed to supervise his teenage son's lawn-cutting job. I have a friend who reminds me I ought to make a list of what I'm going to buy for our dinner. It is as though we were incompetent, this husband and son and I—as though we might make a mistake and that would be *terrible*. Caretakers insist on preventing other people's mistakes. To be fair, sometimes a lot *is* riding on it.

I remember the year our son, Christopher, decided that attending his high school classes was strictly optional. He much preferred going to the movies, walking on the beach, or hanging out at McDonald's with his friends. By the time Bill and I became aware of Christopher's new agenda, he had accumulated nine unexcused absences in his first-hour English class. Ten unexcused absences meant failure for the year and would require him to take eleventh-grade English in summer school or night school in order to graduate.

I panicked. Christopher didn't. Bill and I discussed it with him, and he seemed cheerfully nonchalant. Until then Christopher had been pretty consistent about getting himself up for school. But codependent caretaker that I am, I began making *sure* he got out of bed on time every day so he wouldn't miss that fateful first-hour English class.

Then one day it hit me. Why was I worried? I wouldn't have to go to summer school—I already had my diploma. Why was I doing for Christopher what he could and should be doing for himself? I decided to talk with him about it.

"Christopher, you'll be on your own soon, and I won't be there to wake you up in the morning. From now on you have to get yourself up on time. If you miss your bus and don't make it to school, the consequences are your responsibility."

I watched Christopher's eyes widen as the realization began to sink in. Suddenly concerned, he pleaded, "Mom, could you wean me off slowly from depending on you?"

I agreed to allow him one emergency wake-up call. He used it within a week. For several mornings after that I'd lie in bed forcing myself not to get up and check on Christopher's progress, treating him instead like the responsible young adult I wanted him to become. And believe it or not, Christopher made it through those last eight weeks of school without once missing his first-hour English class. Of course, there was incentive. Staying out of summer school had become *his* responsibility.

HIGHER STAKES

Sometimes, however, the stakes are immeasurably higher. Sometimes they involve the survival of a job or a reputation or a relationship. I spent years telling Bill how to handle his job so he wouldn't lose it and force us to face financial disaster. I know women who have *stopped* doing that and whose husbands *have* lost their jobs. A man I heard about stopped checking up on his wife as a way to keep her faithful; she's now moved in with her lover. A friend who quit acting as though her husband's emotional equilibrium was her responsibility is now facing divorce. These are high stakes, and somehow caretaking, even if it's patronizing, seems a more attractive alternative. Why stop the warning and crisis prevention and managing and emotional coddling if the consequences can be so dire? Isn't a codependent's control preferable to disaster?

CONTROL VIOLATES FREEDOM AND DIGNITY

One reason rescuing and caretaking are so destructive is that they violate the freedom God created us to enjoy as His image-bearers. Someone has said God is a gentleman; He never forces His way on His friends.

Gerald May touched on this God-given freedom when he said, "God lets us make our own decisions, even at times when we would much prefer to be taken care of. God blesses us with responsibility and the dignity it contains."[2]

In contrast, codependents undermine the competence and accountability of those they rescue and take care of, and it ought not surprise them when others resent the manipulation. Caretaking sabotages the give-and-take of healthy relationships, swinging the power and responsibility toward one partner and leaving the other feeling managed and unfree. Codependents are experts at using, not loving, the people with whom they are in relationship. Their manipulation provides a temporary payback of feeling strong, superior, and indispensable.

MOTIVATED BY FEAR

Codependents operate out of both felt and unacknowledged fear, and their attempts to control others flow from that fear and the dynamics that undergird it. It is a fear for their own inner safety, for the reputation of themselves or their families, for their financial security, for the other person's well-being. It leaves no room for faith—neither faith in God nor faith in the other's ability to choose for himself or herself. Fear cancels out faith.

Paradoxically, the codependent's control is also characterized by a fearful dependence on others: "I can't live without this person's sobriety, loving involvement, faithfulness, etc." An emotional blackmail keeps both partners stuck—the codependent expecting love in exchange for caretaking, the addict giving crumbs of affection in exchange for permission to remain irresponsible.

Codependents intend to obligate the ones they love to appreciate and love them in return for "services rendered." No matter that the love is guilt-ridden or the appreciation grudging—or that resentment is corroding everything. The codependent is out to find some way—any way—to get an emotional return on his or her caretaking investment. In the final analysis, it is an abysmal failure to love.

JESUS AND CONTROL

Though Jesus spent the years of His public ministry meeting the legitimate needs of those who occupied His world, He never forced anyone to believe or obey Him, nor did He ever compromise anyone's responsibility to live with the consequences of his or her choice. When He offered the rich young ruler the way to enter eternal life, He allowed him to choose, even though He loved him (Mark 10:17-22). He felt no compulsion to make the ruler do what was good for him. Likewise, with His closest companions Jesus refused to control. Instead He invited them to choose for themselves. "Who do you say I am?" He asked the Twelve (Matthew 16:15). And when many of His followers deserted Him, He turned to His disciples with the question, "You do not want to leave too, do you?" (John 6:67). The choice was theirs, and they freely decided to believe He was the Messiah and to remain with Him. *Jesus was neither compelled by anyone to act a certain way, nor did He compel anyone else to act a certain way.* Jesus never violated people's right to choose their own behavior, but rather He allowed them to experience the consequences of their free choices. Nowhere is the freeing hand of Jesus seen more clearly than in His relationship with Judas Iscariot. It wasn't just that He could have prevented Judas' betrayal but did not; He even told Judas to hurry with his plan (John 13:27), and He let Judas see His pain when he finally carried it out (Matthew 26:50, Luke 22:48). Jesus freed Judas but did not deliver him from the consequences of his betrayal; Judas chose suicide, and Jesus did not intervene.

Jesus often was saddened by the way His disciples let Him down. But His grieving at the sad state of personal affairs He often encountered during His ministry was "clean" grieving, unadulterated by any compulsion to force His own solutions. He let others make their own choices, and He silently insisted on His own right to make His choices.

SUMMING UP

If freedom is essential to love, then attempted control is essentially a failure to love. Codependents compulsively manipulate the significant persons in their lives, sometimes blatantly (telling them what to do or how to do it), sometimes subtly (making "suggestions" or being "helpful"). But the resentment of the one being rescued or taken care of testifies to the codependent's lack of love and the emotional payback he or she seeks through manipulation. Control helps stanch the codependent's fear and justifies his or her expectation of gratitude or good behavior in exchange for his or her efforts. Sometimes the savior mentality—the need to be needed—just feels good.

Whatever the particulars surrounding these attempts to control, it is reprehensible that codependents continue the rescuing, caretaking, and other strategies that have kept them in charge and relationally "safe." The next chapter will examine the codependent's self-sufficiency, or refusal to risk, in relationships.

QUESTIONS FOR BUILDING COMMUNITY

1. Why do children from abusive (i.e., dysfunctional) families usually develop a strong compulsion to control people and circumstances?
2. How do codependents benefit from their attempts to control? Give some examples.
3. Give an example of rescuing from your own life or from the experience of someone you know well.
4. Give an example of illegitimate caretaking from your own life or from the experience of someone you know well.
5. How are rescuing and caretaking essentially selfish?
6. How did Eli fail to love his sons?
7. From Jesus' parable of the prodigal son in Luke 15:11-32, show how the father did or did not rescue his son; show also how that was loving or unloving.
8. Explain how control and self-aggrandizement relate to the "savior complex" of many codependents.

NOTES
1. This illustration was offered by Dr. Dan Allender at a seminar entitled "Pursuing Bold Love," held August 9-10, 1990, at Key Biscayne, Florida.
2. Gerald G. May, *Addiction and Grace* (San Francisco: Harper & Row, Publishers, 1988), pages 120-121.

5

SELF-SUFFICIENCY:
DETERMINED TO STAY SAFE

❦

*True spiritual growth is characterized by increasingly deep
risk taking. . . . As we risk believing, and survive, we learn
that what we risked was true. Then, when the next
opportunity for risking comes along, we will find ourselves
a little less fearful. In this way, faith becomes trust.*
GERALD G. MAY
Addiction and Grace

It was storming when Suzanne awoke with a start, uncertain whether
it was her recurring dream, the pounding rain, or some other noise that
had startled her from sleep. She listened intently for any sound from the
children, then sank back onto her pillow next to Walter's undisturbed
frame and breathed a sorrowful sigh. Would she never forget?

It had happened only once that she could remember, yet the details
had begun haunting her dreams after almost two decades. Her father,
uncharacteristically affectionate after a late New Year's Eve party,
approached her eight-year-old body in the darkened bedroom with
soothing words and searching hands—it was a memory Suzanne had
worked hard to forget. But recently sleep was betraying her more and
more often.

Lying quietly so Walter wouldn't wake up, Suzanne felt the
familiar wave of anger washing over her, anger not toward her father—
after all, he'd been *drunk*, she reasoned—but toward her sleeping
husband. "How could I have married so weak a man?" she berated
herself silently. "Why didn't I find someone to match my own strong
personality?"

Growing up in the sixties had been Suzanne's salvation; she could express her unacknowledged fury over the incest in accepted outrage against social ills. Her self-despising was deflected into hating the system so she wouldn't have to look at the deeper issues of her soul. She'd become hard, tough, a warrior for the underdog, a woman who hid her own pain behind a crusader's mask and justified her belligerence by the rightness of her causes. She didn't mourn the loss of her femininity; it had betrayed her once. "But never again," she'd vowed. "Never again!"

And then had come Walter, with his gentle ways and quiet words, an intriguing balance, Suzanne thought, to her own tough strength. He touched something deep in her—her unacknowledged longing for involvement that was both tender and safe—and she'd married him and borne him two children. Along the way she'd also helped him through school and found him his first two jobs, all the while working as a public health nurse and volunteering on behalf of various causes.

But instead of balancing out her toughness, Walter's tenderness and indecisiveness had come to infuriate Suzanne to the point of despair. He was wonderful with the children, but he backed away from Suzanne's deep emotions and powerful tongue, leaving her exquisitely lonely but too humiliated and stubborn to admit it.

Was there a connection, Suzanne wondered, between the recurring dreams about her father and her anxiety that Walter's present job assignment was almost completed? Her father, who had been unavailable at best and sometimes cruel, had wounded her terribly. Would her husband let her down, too? Shoving the dream to the back burner of her mind, Suzanne turned her thoughts toward forming a plan to rescue the family in case Walter couldn't find another job. Whatever happened, she had to be strong. Everything depended on it.

SELF-SUFFICIENCY

Not all sexually abused women become hardened like Suzanne, but all in some way convert their rage and self-contempt into a passionate commitment to never be hurt again. In chapter 3 we dealt with the codependent characteristic of low self-esteem, the negative self-image common to people from addictive or abusive homes. Low self-esteem, motivated at some level by fear of abandonment or rejection, can be debilitating. Yet the flip side of self-contempt is also common to codependents: a self-sufficiency that says, "I'll run my own life and do things my way.

Asking for help is a sign of weakness, and I refuse to appear weak." This determination to appear strong and invulnerable masks more than insecurity, however. There are dynamics even beneath Suzanne's fear of disappointment or exposure that undergird her self-sufficient style of relating to her world—dynamics that will be discussed at length in chapter 10.

Abuse victims aren't the only ones zealous to run their own lives. The Apostle Peter exhibited self-sufficiency throughout Jesus' ministry. Always compulsive, Peter thought he could handle his world by an aggressive, often cocky approach to things. He dared to walk on water, and succeeded (until he took his eyes off Jesus). Presumptuously, he contradicted Jesus' prediction about His coming death and even wielded a sword to defend Him from His own prediction. It was Peter who emphatically assured Jesus that he would never desert Him though all others fled. Peter was a man confident in his own sufficiency, a man who needed the devastating yet gracious look of Jesus' pain after Peter's denial to teach him his own insufficiency. It was not easy for him to admit his need of Jesus' forgiveness in the face of his own deep failure to love. The lessons of grace are never easy.

REFUSAL TO NEED

Codependents typically refuse to let themselves need the freely chosen tender involvement of others. Neediness terrifies them because it wasn't safe to be needy in childhood. Self-sufficiency for some was necessary for survival if one or both parents abandoned them physically, emotionally, or personally. Children like Suzanne become tough when there is abuse, addiction, or codependency in their homes. The little child who is seven going on twenty-three may *have* to be that way to keep the family from falling apart. To be needy instead of strong could literally have meant death for some codependents in their families of origin.

Neediness for some is also shameful. A woman, shamed as a child for being fearful or upset, represses instinctively her anxiety or sadness as an adult. Codependents fight neediness in different ways. Jenny told no one about Brad's drinking. Andrea took pride in handling the stress of an overwhelming caseload at work without complaining. Lois wouldn't risk confronting Allen or asking her pastor for help. Suzanne refused to lean on Walter. Common to the experience of all these codependents is *the refusal to be appropriately needy*, to humbly admit the limitations of being human.

Because of my role as emotional caretaker in my family of origin, I found neediness repulsive. I remember the first time I told Bill I needed his compassionate strength in my life. I thought I would choke. Always before, I'd been like Suzanne, able to be the strong one who gave and never needed. A "spiritual" woman (my goal in life) didn't need others, I thought; her task was to give, not take. When I finally acknowledged I *did* have needs like everyone else, I had to get off my pedestal and welcome myself to the human race. The shame was awful. So was the fear. What if Bill wouldn't "be there" for me? Actually, even deeper than the shame and the fear were subtle dynamics regarding my relationship with God that I couldn't identify at the time. I just knew it was easier to not need, but yielding self-sufficiency was vital to my recovery from codependency, and an important gift to offer Bill as well.

PERFECTIONISM

Another evidence of self-sufficiency is the belief that one must be perfect in order to be approved—by oneself or anyone else. It matters not that perfection is impossible; perfectionists always try harder anyway, often against incredible odds.

Because of their childhood relationships with unpredictable, compulsive people, codependents learn that being "perfect" may mean one thing one day and another thing the next. They drive themselves crazy trying to figure out what the important people in their lives expect from them at any given moment so they can react perfectly. As often as not, they guess wrong and end up "imperfect" despite their best intentions. To make matters worse, they usually feel compelled to please everyone they meet, so they train themselves to be "psychic" in order to never disappoint anyone.

Another hindrance to perfectionism is the chaos that generally reigns in an addictive or compulsive household. Confusion makes perfectionists feel "nuts" and sabotages their desperate attempts to control the approval of others. In fact, the attempts sometimes get lost in the confusion and have no impact at all on the situation. Jenny tried to be the perfect wife and mother, but Brad was often too drunk to notice and the girls too busy with their own agendas to appreciate her efforts.

Perhaps the saddest thing about perfectionism is that it's a facade, an attempt to make life well ordered and attractive on the outside, even though everything is messy and out of control on the inside. The externally perfect life is an illusion, a false image of togetherness the codependent desperately wants to believe and wants others to believe in order to avoid the pain of reality. And like any other compulsion, perfectionism drives its devotee to ever more desperate levels of trying and failing, until finally nothing works anymore. Being perfect just won't happen.

Though perfectionism sometimes passes as Christian piety, it is evidence not of gratitude toward God nor love for others but a fear of failure and arrogant pride. It demonstrates, in fact, an attitude toward God and others that comes closer to rage than fear, and it always does damage. Perfectionism negates grace and uses other people for its own ends. Robert McGee said that perfectionists "have a compelling desire to be in control of every situation. . . . And woe to the poor soul who gets in the way! . . . People who are driven to succeed use practically everything and everybody to meet that need."[1] Perfectionism and self-sufficiency go hand in hand. Both have at their core this belief: I will make my life work by myself, and I'll come out looking good no matter what the cost to myself or anyone else.

REFUSAL TO RISK

Alongside the codependent's refusal to need and attempts at perfectionism is his or her fearful refusal to take risks. "The human condition is not zero-risk."[2] Jesus declared that if we will not lose our lives (i.e., risk letting go of our idolatrous notions of where life is to be found), we won't find life at all (Matthew 10:39). Staying safe by attempting self-sufficiency has serious consequences spiritually as well as relationally.

It's scary to offer ourselves to another human being. We might be scorned, rejected, or (perhaps worst of all) ignored. Of course, we can't genuinely love someone without offering ourselves, either, so the codependent is caught in a no-win dilemma: risk loving and most likely be hurt, or withhold oneself and stay safe and lonely.

Taking risks is the doorway to freedom, but it feels like the doorway to death for the codependent. Driven by a compulsion to never rock the boat or upset the status quo, codependents can't be spontaneous, or carefree, or wrong. They're not free themselves, nor can they offer freedom to others—who might also rock the boat or upset the status quo. The norm might be painful but at least it's predictable, and unpredictability threatens the illusion of self-sufficiency. *Rather than risk change and healing, the codependent will rigidly cling to what is familiar, even if it is destroying everybody.*

ISOLATION

Another aspect of the codependent's self-sufficiency is isolation. Just as the alcoholic or addict turns increasingly inward and avoids contact with others who might threaten the addiction, so the codependent tends to shun those who might see what is really going on and challenge it. This "closed system" mentality is related to loyalty issues (not revealing family secrets) and to control issues ("I can handle this myself").

The codependent is bound to an unspoken code of secrecy about the family's dysfunction. No one but Jenny's closest sister knew about Brad's drinking, and Suzanne wouldn't have considered talking to anyone about her childhood incest. The loyalty imperative in an abusive family is incredibly strong. Sometimes the threats about "telling" are clear, sometimes only implied. Often the shame is so great *no one* in the family will deal with the problem, let alone talk to anyone else about it. Isolation includes not just secrecy, but also avoiding involvement with anyone who might discover the secret if he or she got close enough. Social interaction, even with extended family members is increasingly constricted in abusive or codependent homes, and the possibility for outside help—for someone to find out and somehow stop the insanity—is diminished to hopelessness.

Isolation is also a control issue. Letting others in on what's happening behind the carefully maintained propriety masking the dysfunction would be tantamount to admitting things are out of control, that these individuals are unable to manage their lives effectively. Thus codependents become experts at isolation as a strategy for looking good, for supporting the illusion of normalcy. Their reputations and sometimes their lives depend on it.

INABILITY TO RECEIVE LOVE, INTIMACY, OR FORGIVENESS

One of the truly sad things about self-sufficiency is that the rigidity sabotages our purpose as God's image-bearers: to love and to be loved by God and others. Codependents who cut themselves off from dependence on God and interdependence with others subvert the very relationships they crave. Intimacy involves risk and a willingness to trust others, but codependents would rather depend on their own resources. They'll settle for being needed rather than risk being hurt, though it leaves them unable to be real, unable to give or receive love, unable to offer forgiveness to themselves or anyone else. What they want they cannot have because it cannot be self-generated. *Sacrificing love, intimacy, and forgiveness is the price they pay for staying safe by staying in charge.*

SPIRITUAL STERILITY

Ironically, self-sufficiency is ultimately an illusion. A. W. Tozer rightly declared, "To stay alive every created thing needs some other created thing and all things need God. To God alone nothing is necessary."[3] To think any person could be self-sufficient is ludicrous, yet that is what codependents are determined to become. And in their attempts to be self-sufficient, they cut themselves off from the very Source who offers both life and purpose. They lose touch with the Power beyond themselves who can breathe life into their souls, and their spirits die within them. Without God and without hope in this world, they live as empty shells, devoid of grace and spiritually bereft. Their spiritual loneliness, if they acknowledge it, haunts their nights and makes a mockery of their frantic days.

WAS JESUS SELF-SUFFICIENT?

Of all the people who ever lived, Jesus of Nazareth had the most right to claim self-sufficiency. He didn't have to need anyone or anything. The Son of Man, the very Word of God made flesh, had life within Himself. The Apostle John declared, "In him was life" (John 1:4).

Yet we find Jesus saying and living out just the opposite of self-sufficiency. He was unafraid to need. He acknowledged without apology that He depended utterly on the Father for everything—from His actions to His very words. The times He spent in private prayer with His Father were not dutiful but life-sustaining. Surely He is appalled at our stubborn refusal to desperately need the Father. Self-sufficiency is not merely an affront to God, but utter foolishness, the equivalent of deliberately choosing death over life.

Jesus also put Himself in a place where, as a man, He needed others as well. He needed His mother, Mary, to care for His physical needs as an infant and child. He accepted the ministry (financial and physical) of the women who followed Him and His disciples. He was unembarrassed to need the companionship of friends, particularly His disciples, creating opportunities to be with them and asking them to pray for Him, especially as He faced His greatest agony in Gethsemane. He risked loving a man He knew would betray Him, and He refused to isolate Himself from even the most critical of His questioners. Confident that His Father would never let Him down, Jesus gladly leaned His full weight on the Father's sufficiency, not His own.

SUMMING UP

Self-sufficiency, the conviction that we must be a strength unto ourselves and can make it on our own, is deeply ingrained in codependent thinking. It exhibits itself in a refusal to need others, perfectionism, an unwillingness to take risks in relationships, and a commitment to isolate ourselves from those who might offer help. Though self-sufficiency sabotages intimacy, most codependents prefer the safety of charting their own course over the messy business of change and freedom in relationships. But to maintain their dangerously flawed belief that they can manage their world through their own efforts, addicts and codependents alike must deny the reality of their situation (past and present), their feelings, and the consequences of their wrong behavior on themselves and those they love. Denial will be the topic of the final chapter in this section.

QUESTIONS FOR BUILDING COMMUNITY

1. How was Suzanne's childhood sexual abuse related to her self-sufficiency?
2. Why is neediness often terrifying or repugnant to codependents?

3. Explain how perfectionism and other forms of self-sufficiency represent a profound failure to love. Give some examples.
4. What function does isolation serve for the addict or codependent?
5. Explain how self-sufficiency sabotages spiritual vitality.
6. In what ways does Jesus' life teach us that self-sufficiency is wrong and futile?
7. Show how self-sufficiency is evident in the case study stories of codependents we've looked at:
   a. Jenny and Brad
   b. Andrea
   c. Lois and Joe
   d. Suzanne and Walter
8. What evidence can you give of self-sufficiency in your own life? Explain why you developed that self-sufficiency and give some examples of how it has led to each of the following:
   a. refusal to need others,
   b. perfectionism,
   c. refusal to risk,
   d. inability to receive love, intimacy, or forgiveness,
   e. spiritual sterility.

NOTES
1. Robert S. McGee, *The Search for Significance* (Houston, TX: Rapha Publishing, 1987), page 26.
2. John De Luca, as quoted by Matthew Purdy in "Alcohol: The Drug Left Out of the President's War," *The Miami Herald* (December 25, 1989), page 1B.
3. A. W. Tozer, *The Knowledge of the Holy* (San Francisco: Harper & Row, Publishers, 1961), pages 39-40.

6

SELF-DECEPTION: COMMITTED TO DENIAL

❦

Denial is the common currency
of troubled families.
JAEL GREENLEAF
"Co-alcoholic/Para-alcoholic: Who's Who?"
in Co-dependency

Robert is an older man with a gentle spirit and a charming wife, Janet. They never had children. Robert is the eldest of four children born of a strict, religious man and a passive, sickly woman. Throughout his life he'd been unable to please his stern, demanding father, who would periodically "binge" on uncontrollable rages with Robert taking the brunt of it. Even as an adult he would receive monthly phone calls from his father and listen to hour-long diatribes against his character, job performance, and personal ability. Robert couldn't bring himself to just hang up; it was his only link to his father. But because of the verbal abuse, Robert believed that the important people in his life could never think well of him.

To offset the pain of being unable to win his father's approval, Robert became "too nice," selling his integrity for the sake of other people's affirmation. Unconsciously he was driven to prove his father wrong and win his father's love after all the years of neglect and abuse. Robert took the blame for whatever went wrong on his job, even when it was clearly someone else's fault, because he wanted his coworkers to like him. He was always the first to apologize, especially with Janet. His motto was *peace at any cost*.

Robert was not a risker. Careful never to put himself in a position where he might look bad, this man missed out on much good he could have done if he had dared try. He narrowed his boundaries to include only what he could do well, closing his eyes to his giftedness and closing the door on opportunities to develop those gifts. He wouldn't involve himself in any of his church's programs because he refused to see himself as competent or significant to people.

Robert's words about himself were consistently negative, even in those circumstances when he had genuinely succeeded. He looked humble and self-sacrificing, but in fact Robert was deeply angry about being devalued. He turned his unacknowledged anger inward, believing himself worthless and becoming ruthlessly self-contemptuous. *His "humble" spirit didn't flow from a position of godly strength, but from a failure to face either his pain or his sin.* Robert was a man unaware of how he'd been damaged and unwilling to face his underlying quiet rebellion against God.

CODEPENDENCY MAINTAINED BY DENIAL

Denial in dysfunctional families refers to the failure or refusal to face honestly what *is* in any given situation or relationship—a "refusal to admit the truth or reality."[1] My pastor, Steve Brown, would challenge me when I came for counseling: "Nancy, tell me what *is*, not what you wish were true or how you think things should be." Denial means we aren't willing to admit what's going on or how bad things really are—or how bad *we* really are.

Denial is learned behavior, especially in troubled families. It happens in two ways and accomplishes two purposes.

CONSPIRACY OF SILENCE

Claudia Black, in her book *It Will Never Happen to Me*, examined the three unspoken rules of a dysfunctional family: *don't talk; don't trust; don't feel.*[2] They are rules about silence, about masking honest appraisals and true feelings regarding what is happening in the family. The conspiracy is not only to remain silent to others but to not even tell oneself the truth.

When parents in an addictive or abusive family conspire to avoid reality, their children conspire with them. They're all ashamed of the drunkenness, eating binges, battering, or pornography, but no one dares mention it, let alone challenge it. Eventually the shame transfers from "this is what's happening" to "this is who my family is" or "this is who I am," and the reasons for denial intensify. Fear that someone will discover the truth and expose the shame dominates the mood of the home. Denial becomes entrenched, and the children (like their parents) refuse to look at, talk about, or deal with the family's secrets.

The "don't talk" rule does great damage, especially to the children. Family loyalty becomes synonymous with never discussing the family's problems, even as siblings within the home. I was in my forties before I talked with my brother and sisters about my father's alcoholism and my mother's codependency—and even then we felt disloyal. We had tacitly agreed to keep silence those many years, short-circuiting the understanding and grace we might have offered one another had we felt free to address reality.

Denial does much to sustain an addictive or abusive family system. It also perpetuates the system because an unexamined pattern of abuse repeats itself, making the abuse multigenerational. The rules of silence remain in place until someone dares to challenge the system and open the door to change.

Denial of the Problem

The first level of denial is an unwillingness to admit there even is a problem in the family. Jenny and Brad both denied his drinking was disruptive. Andrea was unaware of her codependency, and Joe and Lois were loathe to admit Allen's drug problem. Suzanne worked hard to obliterate the memory of her childhood abuse. Robert refused to believe his father had damaged him.

The drinking, incest, workaholism, drug dependency, mental illness, or codependency may be obvious to everyone else, but the family members simply refuse to admit anything is abnormal. To them the dysfunctional home *is* normal, even if miserable. Things that don't seem normal to the child at first—like daddy lying drunk in the front yard or mommy slumped in a chair dissolved in tears—are explained away as normal ("Daddy is camping" or "Mommy's stomach hurts"). Eventually the child doesn't trust his or her own perceptions anymore, and denial about how crazy things are becomes second nature.

But codependents don't just deny the reality of addiction or abuse. They also ignore the problems that come from dysfunction. The codependent compulsively engages in *magical thinking*, the unfounded expectation that the addiction-related difficulties will somehow improve by themselves—the alcoholic will quit drinking, the pornographer will throw away his books and tapes, the daughter will stop binging or start eating, the parent will begin spending less time at work and more time at home, the addicted wife will find a job and quit using, the husband will stop beating his wife and kids. Somehow the bills will be paid, the runaway will come home, the yard will get mowed, the spouse will become faithful, the children will no longer have problems at school, the broken bones will stop hurting. To maintain the illusion of normalcy, the codependent often must deny not only the primary problem of addiction or abuse but also the secondary problems, both practical and relational, that flow out of the addiction or abuse.

Denial of Emotions

There is a second level of denial that exists beneath the codependent's denial about family problems, both primary and secondary. In discussing this level of denial, Jael Greenleaf stated, "Concomitant with denial of the problem is denial of the feelings that the problems produce."[3] This more basic level of denial involves repression, the refusal to allow oneself to feel the negative feelings associated with what's happening in the family. Jenny and her daughters didn't let themselves feel angry about Brad's behavior, nor did Suzanne or Robert open themselves to the pain of their fathers' abusiveness. Andrea couldn't believe she resented being used by her friends, and Lois refused to face her rage at both Joe and Allen. The masks of frozen feelings these codependents hid behind served to keep them safe from reality and the frightening consequences of becoming honest.

Codependents don't merely believe the negative emotions will go away if ignored. They also fear the emotions will get out of hand if released. Their rage (which may not yet be felt consciously) against God and against those who have abused or betrayed them might break out into open revenge and destroy many. Their loved ones would surely abandon or abuse them if they made known their true feelings. They fear that even God might leave.

In the face of incontrovertible evidence, codependents are able to deny how bad things are and how angry and frightened they feel. Their children and colleagues often cooperate in the charade. It's safer to pretend, to minimize the extent or consequences of the problem. Ten years of denial passed from the time I sat on that rock in the Florida Keys knowing Bill had a drinking problem until I attended my first support-group meeting for families of substance abusers. And it took an additional three years of support-group work before I could say without flinching that Bill is an alcoholic. He didn't believe he was, and I wanted to believe him. The deception of denial is incredibly strong.

USEFULNESS OF DENIAL

Denial serves many purposes, but there are two general categories of usefulness. Pretense about "what is" projects a favorable image (especially in the church) and protects us from the pain of disappointing circumstances and relationships. Let's examine these two functions of denial.

Impression Management
One of the most powerful motivators in today's society is the desire to look good. No one likes to fail, but codependents can't live with themselves unless they're universally admired. Impression management holds top priority for codependents, who try to manage their world, their circumstances, and their emotions so as to convince others that their homes are happy and their relationships are functioning well. They are less concerned with how they really feel than with how they ought to feel or how others want them to feel. Andrea, for example, wants to impress others as a woman who can handle any stress or pain. So she must pretend she is never too tired, never too confused, never too "selfish" to drop whatever she's doing to meet someone else's needs. If she were to look at her true feelings—her anger at being used, her sadness at being ignored, her resentment against her supervisor—the impression she wants to make would suffer and she would feel ashamed and inadequate. So she maintains the ego facade and manages to sustain (for a while) the image of the selfless worker.

Denial also keeps us from seeing our own love failures. When Andrea faces her true emotions, she will have to acknowledge that her real goal has been her own self-protection, not ministry to others. She has wanted to look good more than she has wanted to offer her true self to others for their good. Impression management is not just deceitful, it's also unloving.

The cost of impression management is high. The relentless fear that the facade might fail and reveal the real person inside inevitably takes its toll. Codependents support their addictive habit with physical payments for their stuffed emotions—ulcers, colitis, migraines, and arthritis, to name a few. Emotionally they pay, too. Loneliness, bitterness, and failure to genuinely enjoy relationships are just some of the negative consequences of impression management. Relationally, codependents find that shallow friendships are all that's available when they're committed to emotional disguising.

But the codependent in denial does get to avoid looking at the mess inside, which brings us to the second major function of denial: protection from the pain of looking within.

Protection from Pain

When codependents polish the exterior while refusing to examine the interior of their lives, they can put off for a time the painful reality of what is inside—the character flaws, the disappointment about past or present relationships, the failures to love, the lost opportunities, the shattered dreams, the deep loneliness. Denial functions well to keep codependents from facing that inner pain.

Timmen Cermak said it this way:

Denial stems from an internal preoccupation with avoiding pain. It is like a flashlight that works in reverse, casting shadows rather than light. It throws darkness over selected parts of the world to make them less noticeable, enabling us to hide embarrassing parts of our personality from our own vision, even though these parts may be obvious to everyone else. . . . Denial prevents us from seeing things that make us too uncomfortable.[4]

If codependents are to face life as it really is and make the inner changes that will genuinely transform their lives, they will have to drop the protection denial affords them from the pain of an inside look.

KING IN DENIAL

One of the saddest biblical examples of a man committed to denial is King David. Though he was truly a man after God's own heart, David, in his later years, failed profoundly to face and deal with the weaknesses of his children.

The unhappy story is recorded in 2 Samuel 13–19. It began when David's eldest son and heir, Amnon, raped his beautiful half sister Tamar. Disgraced and now unmarriageable, Tamar moved into her brother Absalom's home. Though her father, David, was furious, he denied the atrocity by neither rebuking nor punishing Amnon for his blatant immorality against Tamar.

But Absalom did not forget. He brooded for two years, planning and then executing the death of Amnon in revenge for his sister's violation. Absalom had to run for his life and remained in exile for three years, hearing nothing from his father, David. Again David chose denial and inaction instead of dealing forthrightly with Absalom's murder of Amnon. It was as though Absalom's physical absence from Jerusalem allowed David to close his eyes to the pain of having "lost" both sons. David simply would not look at or deal with the chaos in his family life.

After David finally allowed Absalom to return to Jerusalem, two years passed before he allowed his son to enter his presence, and even then he did not deal with Absalom's sin. Absalom had returned unrepentant, bitter about David's failure to deal with Amnon and about his own five-year banishment from his father's presence. Once more David had failed to deal with the "what is" in his family.

In the end David reaped terrible consequences from his denial about his sons' sins and his unwillingness to face his responsibility as both father and king to deal justly with them. Absalom later attempted a political coup, instigated a civil war in Israel, slept publicly with his father's concubines, and eventually met a violent death. These circumstances had been foretold by the prophet Nathan as judgment against David for his earlier sin with Bathsheba (2 Samuel 12:10-12). A footnote in *The NIV Study Bible* suggests a connection between David's refusal to confront Absalom with his sin and the later tragedy that befell the entire nation: "David sidesteps repentance and justice, and in this way he probably contributes to the fulfillment of the prophecy of Nathan."[5]

The king's refusal to look at his problem or his pain proved disastrous for his family and for the whole nation of Israel.

NEGATIVE CONSEQUENCES OF DENIAL

Denial is not simply a benign option for dealing with life's problems. As seen in David's life, the consequences of denial are far-reaching and devastating. Denial destroys a person's relationships, resulting in spiritual sterility in relationship to God, loss of authenticity in relationship to oneself, and absence of intimacy in relationships with others.

Spiritual Sterility

Children who learn to cope with life through denial instead of acknowledging their sin and leaning on God as they work through the pain in their lives often grow up to become adults unconnected to the God they were created to enjoy. Their spiritual impoverishment exhibits itself in many ways, but its primary evidence is their superficial walk with God. I grew up in a decidedly religious environment, but my relationship with God was cerebral and distant; I hid my true self—both my pain and my anger—from Him as I had hidden it from everyone, including myself. Denial kept me "safe" from God by keeping me from a desperate dependence on His grace that would surely have deepened communion between us. I suspect my experience is common to most codependents.

Loss of Authenticity

A second consequence of denial is the codependents' loss of authenticity in relationship to themselves. Refusing to look honestly at "what is" makes people strangers to themselves, unaware of their true feelings, failings, and needs. They become empty shells, reacting superficially to the people who occupy their lives.

Codependents in denial also fail to believe or enjoy their own value and impact as persons of worth. Thinking themselves worthless, they refuse to genuinely offer the deep part of themselves to others.

Absence of Intimacy

A third consequence flows naturally out of the second: When we are strangers to ourselves, we cannot disclose ourselves to others, and the result is an absence of intimacy in even our closest relationships. A friend once asked me, "How long do you think my husband has been a stranger to me?" I replied, "He's been a stranger to himself—to his own motives, emotions, and needs—most of his life. How can he reveal himself to you when he doesn't know who he is himself?"

It's impossible to share what we don't know. Until we reach in to enter our own pain and joy, we can't reach out to share someone else's pain or joy. If we can't be real about ourselves, we can't be real with anyone else. The basis for genuine intimacy is genuine honesty. Denial sabotages both.

Perhaps most seriously, denial keeps people from being honest about how they have wounded others and rebelled against God. Denial about their own flaws, love failures, and anger prevents the very intimacy their souls long for from God and others, an intimacy that can come only through being deeply known and exposed and then forgiven and embraced. Denial prevents repentance and resists grace.

JESUS AND DENIAL

Jesus, the perfect human being, never denied what *was* in His life. He always squarely faced His circumstances, even when they were terrible. When He began teaching His disciples about His approaching death, "Peter took him aside and began to rebuke him. 'Never, Lord!' he said. 'This shall never happen to you!'" (Matthew 16:22). Peter tried to force Jesus into denial of the awful truth by urging his own perception of reality. But Jesus resisted, choosing instead to look at reality without flinching and calling Peter's "optimism" satanic (Matthew 16:23).

Nor did Jesus fall into denial about His pain. He never masked His true feelings but expressed them openly and without shame. He wept at Lazarus's grave, verbalized His frustration at the Pharisees' hypocrisy, expressed His anger by overturning the tables of the moneychangers and temple merchants, agonized to the point of sweating blood when facing His own death in Gethsemane, and finally gave up His life with a loud scream. His was the most consistently authentic life ever lived.

SUMMING UP

Like all codependent characteristics, denial is rooted not just in fear but also in rebellion against God. It reflects a misunderstanding of grace and a failure to live by that grace. God knows our hearts, and He knows codependency's strong hold on our lives. He desires us to face it squarely, not to shame us but to free us from the prisons we've been living in for too long. He longs for us to abandon our nonauthentic Christian lives built on pretense and self-protection and live instead in honesty and grace, which is impossible until we admit the bondage.

We've examined in this first section five characteristics of codependency: *self-forfeiture, self-contempt, self-aggrandizement, self-sufficiency,* and *self-deception.* Different codependents emphasize different characteristics, depending on their individual temperaments, upbringing, and life situations. But the common thread that runs through them all is self-preoccupation. Codependents are focused on themselves, on getting their own needs met in whatever way has worked for them in the past. Consider again the definition of codependency from chapter 1:

> *Codependency is a self-focused way of life in which a person blind to his or her true self continually reacts to others, being controlled by and seeking to control their behavior, attitudes and/or opinions, resulting in spiritual sterility, loss of authenticity, and absence of intimacy.*

Though the codependent's behaviors often look unselfish, at the core they're intended to keep the codependent in charge and out of personal pain.

Codependency operates out of a determined demandingness that others affirm and please the codependent. This demandingness can be quiet or unruly, pleasant or ugly, passive or aggressive, sweet or abrasive. But however it plays itself out, the internal dynamics of codependency are deeply self-centered. The next section will examine the development of codependency as a way of life that violates God's offer of genuine life in Christ, which makes it possible for us to love Him above all and to love others as ourselves.

QUESTIONS FOR BUILDING COMMUNITY

1. Why is denial important to the members of abusive or addictive families?
2. What are the negative consequences of denial in these areas:

    a. spiritual (relationship with God),

    b. personal (relationship with self),

    c. relational (relationship with others).

3. What would it have cost David to have come out of denial about the abuse in his family from the beginning (by dealing with Amnon's sin)?

4. How do "frozen feelings" keep codependents from being fully engaged in relationships? How does denial sabotage genuine Christian fellowship?

5. Think of an instance when Jesus confronted people with the reality of:
    a. their pain (disappointment),
    b. their sin.

6. How did Jesus' refusal to deny the reality of pain or sin lead to blessing for the people involved?

7. Briefly describe one incident from your childhood you would most like to ignore or forget.
    a. How would your life be different if you could forget it?
    b. How might denial be useful to you regarding that memory?
    c. What might be the benefit of renouncing denial and facing the memory with honesty and integrity?

NOTES

1. *Webster's New Collegiate Dictionary* (Springfield, MA: G. & C. Merriam Company, 1980), page 300.

2. Claudia Black, *It Will Never Happen to Me* (Denver, CO: M.A.C. Printing and Publications Division, 1981), chapter 3.

3. Jael Greenleaf, "Co-alcoholic/Para-alcoholic: Who's Who?" *Co-dependency* (Deerfield Beach, FL: Health Communications, Inc., 1984), page 9.

4. Timmen L. Cermak, *A Time to Heal* (Los Angeles, CA: Jeremy P. Tarcher, Inc., 1988), pages 33-34.

5. *The NIV Study Bible* (Grand Rapids, MI: Zondervan Corporation, 1988), footnote to 2 Samuel 14:33, page 446.

PART TWO

WHERE DOES BONDAGE COME FROM?

7

FERVENT LONGINGS

❧

We are dependent by nature. We require resources
outside ourself if we're to enjoy either physical
or personal life. . . . God intended that we warmly
respond to the loving strength of another, and what we
were built to enjoy, we deeply desire.
LARRY CRABB
Inside Out

The first section of this book described codependency as a self-focused way of life that keeps us from genuine freedom in relationships. The question is, Can a person move away from codependency? Is recovery possible?

It's not enough to simply tell someone (or oneself) to stop being codependent. As in other compulsions, willpower alone does not effect long-term, lasting change. Behavior adjustments ("Stop doing this" or "Start doing that") must happen, but they are not enough. Nor are compulsions managed through environmental rearrangements, such as moving to a new place or finding new friends. Something deeper is required, something on the inside. The codependent must experience a revolutionary new look at what life is and how it is to be lived, particularly in the spiritual dimension.

To embark on the journey of inner change, we must begin with the question of origin. Where does codependency come from and how does it develop? Understanding origins will help shape our journey toward recovery.

To chart a course toward wholeness, it is imperative to define the nature of man (used here to refer to both male and female human beings). What was man created to be and do? What does he need, and what can he give? The Bible has much to say about the nature and purpose of man.

CREATED TO REFLECT GOD

The opening chapters of Genesis tell us that human beings didn't accidentally happen; God created them separate from and superior to the rest of creation. Moses told us,

> Then God said, "Let us make man in our image, in our likeness, and let them rule over the fish of the sea and the birds of the air, over the livestock, over all the earth, and over all the creatures that move along the ground." So God created man in his own image, in the image of God he created him; male and female he created them. (Genesis 1:26-27)

Adam and Eve were to rule over all of God's creation. Moreover, the kind of beings Adam and Eve were reflected the kind of being God is, since they were created in His image. "God is spirit," the Apostle John wrote (John 4:24), and man, too, is spiritual as well as physical. This reality often is denied or ignored as people seek to satisfy the physical, rational, relational, and emotional aspects of their being in a spiritual vacuum. The awakening of a person to his or her spirituality is essential to recovery from codependency.

Longing for Impact

Two other things must be said about the nature of man, both having to do with what man was created to desire. The first has been alluded to already. Man was created to long for and seek after productivity and impact. The "cultural mandate" God gave Adam and Eve in Genesis 1:28 reflects their innate need to make a difference in their world: "God blessed them and said to them, 'Be fruitful and increase in number; fill the earth and subdue it. Rule over the fish of the sea and the birds of the air and over every living creature that moves on the ground.'" The first thing God did after creating Adam was to give him something to do: to work and protect the Garden of Eden, and to name the animals (Genesis 2:15,19). We were created for impact, impact on our environment and circumstances, and impact in the lives of others.

Longing for Relationship

That brings us to the second desire of man, the longing for openness and connectedness with other personal beings. God Himself is a personal Being who communes in perfect unity within the Godhead (Father, Son, and Holy Spirit). In considering the creation of man, God said, "Let *us* make man in *our* image, in *our* likeness" (Genesis 1:26, emphasis added). The social interchange and radical other-centeredness within the Trinity models what man is also created for as God's image-bearers. Our relational longings move in two directions: toward God and toward other people.

There was from the beginning an ongoing relationship between God and man. God spoke to Adam (2:16) and later to Adam and Eve together (3:8-10). We have few details about the pre-Fall dialogue between God and man, but it clearly existed. In fact, throughout the biblical narrative God is revealed as pursuing connectedness with men and women, just as they longed for relationship with Him. "As the deer pants for streams of water," the psalmist wrote, "so my soul pants for you, O God. My soul thirsts for God, for the living God" (Psalm 42:1-2). We are built to yearn for relationship with our Creator, to depend on Him, and to bring Him glory.

But we're also built to relate to other people. God declared: "It is not good for the man to be alone. I will make a helper suitable for him" (Genesis 2:18). Then the account follows of how God created Eve and presented her to Adam—thus instituting marriage as God's choice love-gift to His beloved children. The story concluded: "For this reason a man will leave his father and mother and be united to his wife, and they will become one flesh" (2:24). Our longing for relationship with others (particularly in the one-woman-one-man covenant for life) is presented as good and God-given. It's okay to need and depend on other people. In fact, it's more than okay; it is our nature.

APPROPRIATE DEPENDENCIES

Dependence is not a bad thing, particularly dependence on God. A. W. Tozer has said, "The word *necessary* is wholly foreign to God,"[1] but it is wholly natural to man. "Among all created beings, not one dare trust in itself. God alone trusts in Himself; all other beings must trust in Him."[2] Dependence on God is what we were created for; it is, in fact, the only way we can experience genuine spiritual vitality. Adam and Eve's pre-Fall life was intricately bound to their utter and glad dependence on the God from whom that life had come.

But another legitimate dependency also existed in Eden, the mutual interdependence between Adam and Eve. It was appropriate for them to depend on each other, to enjoy natural and unashamed give-and-take in their relationship. Mutual interdependence was affirmed by God's creation of both male and female, two beings bound together by need (they were incomplete without each other) and benefaction (they had the capacity to meet each other's need for help and oneness). Those who strive for self-sufficiency and total independence miss the mutuality of interdependence they were created for.

Before the Fall, Adam and Eve enjoyed gladly both their dependence on God and on each other. They lived in a natural and radical other-centeredness, each using his or her own giftedness and personhood to bring blessing to God and one another. Moreover, they experienced from God and each other perfect acceptance and freedom in being who they were. It is what we all long for—to be accepted as we are in any given moment, to be free to not pretend, and to gladly love from a full heart. Their dependencies neither bound nor shamed them, but were instead an accepted and cherished part of their being. What they had to give they freely offered, and what they depended on was unfailingly provided—love and authenticity from both God and one another.

EFFECTS OF THE FALL

Unfortunately, it didn't last. Adam and Eve rebelled against dependence on God in order to become god and goddess of their own lives. They believed Satan's deception that disobedience would make them "like God" (Genesis 3:5). Declaring their independence from God cost them eternal life; they experienced a kind of soul death, becoming separated from both the God who had made them and the partners He had made for them. Impelled now to hide from one another and from Him, they lost the glad dependence they'd enjoyed in their relationships. In its place was fear, separation, loneliness, and self-centeredness.

It wasn't that the dependencies were removed. Adam and Eve still needed God and each other. But they no longer trusted that those dependency needs would be met. Their longings (and ours) remain, but without the assurance of being satisfied. As Dr. Larry Crabb has said, "We long for both respect and involvement, impact and relationship. We are thirsty for what our soul thrives on. In the desert of a fallen world, our soul is parched. We receive neither respect nor involvement to the degree we deeply crave."[3]

Having violated their dependence on God and fearing their mutual interdependence, God's image-bearers now had another need besides the need for acceptance and freedom. They still longed for acceptance and freedom, but conditional to that they now also needed forgiveness. Having rebelled against depending on God, we all need forgiveness from Him before we can enjoy relationship with Him. And because we congenitally fail to satisfy one another's legitimate dependency needs, we must receive and offer forgiveness to others as well if we are to live together in acceptance and authenticity. Appropriate dependence on God and others is still possible, but what is natural to man since the Fall is self-sufficiency (rebellion against God-dependence) and self-centeredness (refusal to meet each others' needs).

FORMING APPROPRIATE DEPENDENCIES IN CHILDHOOD

Even in a fallen world, however, we are called to move toward depending on God and others in the way God intended. Ideally it begins with the training of children in one's family of origin. Infants, of course, are totally dependent on their parents or other caregivers. Without physical and emotional nurturing babies die. Their dependency is not wrong or shameful. God intended parents to meet the needs of the very young—not just the physical necessities, but the personal and emotional needs for connectedness and impact as well. It is the responsibility and privilege of parents to give their children the love, respect, responsibility, and affirmation they need as they develop into mature adults.

However, parents are also called to help their children transfer their obedience and legitimate dependency needs to God Himself. God said about Abraham: "I have chosen him, so that he will direct his children and his household after him to keep the way of the LORD by doing what is right and just" (Genesis 18:19). Later He told the Israelites through Moses: "These commandments that I give you today are to be upon your hearts. Impress them on your children. Talk about them when you sit at home and when you walk along the road, when you lie down and when you get up" (Deuteronomy 6:6-7). As parents respond to their children's dependency, they must also consistently point their children to obedience and trust in God, recognizing that He alone can meet a person's deepest spiritual needs.

Thus, if children have healthy parenting during their early years, they move away from their total dependence on their parents and learn to develop other appropriate dependencies. They learn about trusting God to "be there" for them, and they learn what it means to live in community with others—at home, at school, at church, and in the neighborhood. These lessons in mutual interdependence are sometimes taught by the parents, but they are more often "caught" by the children through the way parents model their own God-dependence and interdependence with others.

By the time children reach adolescence, they are ready to increasingly break from total dependence on their parents and transfer their dependencies to God and to appropriate give-and-take relationships with others in their own way and time. The break is sometimes difficult on both sides, but ideally parents will allow children to determine their own relationship with God and to form friendships based on what has been modeled during the eighteen or so years at home. It is not that children will learn to be independent, but that they will transfer legitimate dependency needs to God and to mutually loving relationships with their peers (as well as to others with whom they must relate). Their dependency is not abandoned, but redirected.

NO GUARANTEES

One of the great difficulties of living in a post-Eden world is that, as children and as adults, our need for connectedness with God is not perfectly met. The fault is not in God, of course; He is ever ready to meet us at every point of need. The problem lies in the fact that as fallen human beings (even as *forgiven* human beings) our capacity to experience His acceptance and grace is impaired by nature and by habit. We cannot sustain unbroken fellowship with Him until we're Home. Our tastes of dependent communion with God in this life are sweet but incomplete; they always leave us yearning for more.

There are no guarantees that our longings for impact, acceptance, and freedom will be met in our relationships with others, either. In fact, because we live in a fallen world, we experience the legitimate fear (even certainty) that our longings for connectedness *won't* be met—certainly not perfectly nor all the time. At best, mutual interdependence is difficult to achieve; at worst, it is sometimes altogether unavailable.

That leaves us with a difficult decision. What are we going to do with our unsatisfied longings for acceptance and freedom? Especially for children who grew up in dysfunctional or abusive homes, the problem of unmet dependency needs is excruciating. In fact, as we shall see more clearly in the chapters to come, addiction and codependency have to do with *misplaced dependencies* for satisfying unmet longings for acceptance and connectedness with God and others. Dependency doesn't go away; it just gets redirected—and more often than not, misdirected.

SUMMING UP

As we seek to satisfy our deep desire for acceptance and freedom, we must remember that the longings themselves are God-given. A common strategy for avoiding the pain of unmet dependency needs is to deaden our longings for what we may never receive. It's safer to not need God or others than to face the possibility (even likelihood) that we might not find the depth of love and impact we so desperately crave. Denial functions well to disacknowledge both the unmet need for connectedness and the addiction or codependency that attempts to mask the painful loss of that connectedness. Then it's just one more step to deny the anger, sorrow, guilt, and fear that accompany the loss. Killing the longing for intimate relationships sometimes just seems to make sense.

What we often don't realize, however, is that denying or killing our deepest longings leaves us spiritually destitute and closed to connecting with God on a level that offers us our only hope for joy and meaning. When we refuse to feel the ache of our longings, we close the one avenue we have toward having them met.

If there is to be healing for codependency, it must begin by affirming the legitimacy of our longings for forgiveness, acceptance, and freedom in our relationships with God and others. Though it will plunge us into the painful reality of those longings having been imperfectly met (or possibly even abused), we must reclaim our birthright of God-dependence and mutual interdependence. If we don't, we can never experience the bittersweet joy of living as we were created to live. We are built for acceptance and freedom in relationships. To try to live without longing for those things may spare us a certain amount of raw pain, but we will ultimately be left hollow at our core, and we will not fulfill the central purpose for which we were created: to love God and others with all our heart, soul, mind, and strength. A deadened heart cannot love or be loved with any integrity at all.

Before we can open ourselves anew to longing and loving, we need to understand more of what lies behind our tendency to remain closed and in denial. The next chapter will explore the process of facing our disappointment at having legitimate dependency needs that were imperfectly met.

QUESTIONS FOR BUILDING COMMUNITY

1. What does the Creation story in Genesis teach us about the nature of man?
2. Explain the difference between man's longing for impact and man's longing for relationship.
3. Name some ways we refuse to depend on God.
4. Is it true that if we could have a close enough relationship with God we wouldn't need other people? Why, or why not?
5. What makes our longings for relationships feel so risky and dangerous?
6. Why do codependents often kill their longings for impact and for relationship?
7. What are some ways in which you or someone you know well have killed your longings for intimacy?
8. What are some negative consequences of squelching our longings for impact and relationship? What are some positive consequences for allowing those longings to surface and thrive?

NOTES

1. A. W. Tozer, *The Knowledge of the Holy* (San Francisco: Harper & Row, Publishers, 1961), page 40.
2. Tozer, page 42.
3. Larry Crabb, *Inside Out* (Colorado Springs, CO: NavPress, 1988), page 70.

8

PAINFUL LOSSES

❧

*We are raising a whole generation of children who are
victims of "the unattached child syndrome." They have
never been truly "bonded" with their parents and,
unless this is healed and changed, they will never get
close to anyone.*
DAVID A. SEAMANDS
Healing Grace

Children come into the world with yearnings for relationship and impact that they unabashedly insist others satisfy for them. As babies they expect their parents to be at their beck and call to provide the necessities of life. That infantile demandingness is legitimate; if their parents fail, the children have no other resources by which to survive.

Adults, too, long for intimacy and impact in relationships, and those longings are good, not shameful. Reclaiming our God-given yearnings is essential if they have been repressed or denied.

But affirming our legitimate longings is only the first step. It's also necessary to acknowledge the degree to which those dependencies were inadequately met in our families of origin. All parents are imperfect, and thus all children are to a greater or lesser degree imperfectly nurtured. Children's nurturing losses, combined with their own fallen natures, damage their ability to love well.

DAMAGE THROUGH NEGLECT AND ABUSE

God intended that families provide children a safe environment of parental connectedness in which to develop a grace-based view of God, themselves, and others. When a child's family environment is *not* safe but abusive in some way—i.e., when the parental bond is missing or weakened—that child's view of God, self, and others will be distorted and grace will be short-circuited. The loss is often enormous.

Sometimes the deprivation of connectedness between parent and child is extreme. Some homes evidence blatant neglect, where the children's basic physical needs go unmet because of parental immaturity, self-centeredness, mental illness, advanced alcoholism, or some other debilitating addiction.

Equally sad are the homes where abuse occurs. The abuse may be physical (wife-battering and/or child-beating), sexual (physical, visual, or verbal), emotional (the child is shamed out of or forbidden to have or express certain feelings), or mental (twisting of reality or entrenched denial about family secrets). Children are profoundly affected by abuse of any kind. They come to see themselves as responsible for and deserving of the abuse they receive because it is too horrifying for them to view life without their parents as their protectors. Guilt, shame, and low self-esteem always characterize victims of childhood abuse.

Christian families, too, suffer with the reality of neglect and every type of family abuse. For them, it is particularly shameful that their faith and desire to obey God don't seem to "work" in overcoming their secret compulsions. All family members live terrified, not only of the pain of the physical or emotional battering, but also of the shame of exposure.

ABANDONMENT AND ROLE REVERSAL

Another way the legitimate dependency needs of children are not adequately met is through parental abandonment. The primary abandonment image is of an infant left in a basket on someone's doorstep. But parental abandonment can take many forms. John Bradshaw lists several ways parents abandon their children:

1. By actually physically leaving them.
2. By not modeling their own emotions for their children.
3. By not being there to affirm their children's expressions of emotion.
4. By not providing for their children's developmental dependency needs.

5. By physically, sexually, emotionally and spiritually abusing them.
6. By using children to take care of their own unmet dependency needs.
7. By using children to take care of their marriages.
8. By hiding and denying their shame secrets to the outside world so that the children have to protect these covert issues in order to keep the family balance.
9. By not giving them their time, attention and direction.
10. By acting shameless.[1]

An abandoned child suffers profound loss, primarily connected to shame regarding his inner self. The child's belief about his lack of worth becomes entrenched when he suffers the loss of attachment with his parents. "*If they don't love me,*" he subconsciously reasons, "*I must be unlovable.*" And the shame, though repressed, follows him into adulthood. Melody Beattie wrote, "Shame has its roots in our childhood and its branches in our lives today."[2]

Moreover, a kind of role reversal occurs when a child is abandoned. In order to survive the loss of parental grace, the child takes responsibility for caring for his parents, who are too needy to care for him. It is a burden too great for any child to bear, but countless emotionally abandoned children try nevertheless.

Because children have so desperate a need for nurturing, however, they must create a fantasy of connectedness with their parents when little or none is available. In the development of codependency, a fantasy bond—i.e., a fantasy that there is a parent-child bond where in fact none exists, or that the bond is stronger than it actually is—becomes an integral part of the denial system that insulates the codependent from the excruciating pain of reality. And the greater the loss of parental bonding, the greater the children's need to pretend that it did exist. Children experience deep loss and profound anger when their longings for connectedness are not met in their families of origin.

UNACKNOWLEDGED WOUNDEDNESS

However, most children are unable to face or verbalize their anger or sorrow about the loss of nurturing from their parent(s). They don't know how to deal with their unmet dependency needs, and they usually have no one to show them how. A counselor friend of mine wrote about his childhood loss:

> I was raised in a motherless home for the first fifteen years of my life. My mother was mentally ill. I never sat on her lap . . . or munched a warm cookie that she had just baked. I never had Mom wipe away a tear because someone had just called me "fatso." Worst of all, I was made to feel that something was wrong with me because my Mom had this mysterious illness. . . . Not once while I was a child did someone ask me, "How do you feel about your mom's sickness?" or, "How are you doing with your loneliness?"[3]

Children growing up in emotionally nonnurturing homes suffer terrible loneliness and shame, having no idea how to deal with their losses except through self-blame and desperate attempts to restore the family's balance. They remain unaware of the damage done to them by their often unsuspecting parents, though they carry the scars into their adult relationships, particularly through their camouflaged or displaced anger and the negative self-images they retain from childhood.

I certainly was unaware of my own anger and shame resulting from my childhood losses. In fact, I don't remember much at all about my childhood, and I suspect my memory lapse is related somehow to my father's developing alcoholism during those years. I know that by the time I reached adolescence I felt responsible for absorbing and alleviating the emotional chaos intrinsic to an alcoholic family. My own loss of emotional nurturing (because of my family's preoccupation with my parents' problems) was swallowed up by my determination to "fix" the crazy feelings in myself and everyone else in my home.

What further complicates the problem is that the child's devastating loss of emotional nurturing is often unacknowledged or denied, even into adulthood. Codependents in particular cherish an illusion of normalcy about their childhood. This illusion is similar to my fantasy about how secure I felt as a youngster. This illusion is strengthened by loyalty issues, which keep adult children from talking about and questioning the abnormality of their childhood experiences. I was naively unaware of the profound impact my early losses had on all my relationships. Adults who were not touched, held, rocked, protected, praised, or listened to as children are left with gaps in their souls. Their woundedness, if left unacknowledged, will continue to repeat itself and make restoration to community difficult, if not impossible.

The family's conspiracy of silence, however well-intentioned, does great damage through their refusal to ask for help. Often the damage continues unconfronted and is passed to the next generation. My emotional deficit was a legacy my parents had inherited from their own families of origin, a legacy subsequently handed down to me and my siblings as well. Nurturing losses are multigenerational.

LOST CHILDHOOD

The loss of adequate parenting in childhood often leaves wounded adults with a sense of never having had a childhood at all. Expected to be their own (and sometimes their parents') resource for nurturing, abused or neglected children grow up not knowing how to be genuinely carefree, spontaneous, or unencumbered by either parent- or self-imposed responsibilities. Many unnurtured, hurting adults respond to their world as the six- or eight- or eleven-year-olds they are emotionally. As my friend Ron Ross has said, "When I reached adulthood, I was an emotional child trapped in an adult body."[4] People may label these wounded adults immature or selfish, but an equally accurate label may be codependent. These adults are still looking for someone to meet the needs that went unmet in their families of origin.

DEFICIT FROM LOSSES

The gap left in the child's soul because of neglectful or abusive parents centers on the shame of his perception that his real self, his inner person, is unacceptable, not enough, inadequate. When parents fail to minister grace to their children, to esteem and value them as precious for their own sakes, children absorb the shame of their inadequacies into their deepest images of themselves. This shame does damage far beyond the original dysfunction because it is damage they unintentionally continue to perpetrate on themselves. John Bradshaw calls it "a kind of soul murder."[5] When a child's dependency needs are not satisfied by his parents, the damage to his soul is penetrating and long-lasting.

UNACKNOWLEDGED ANGER

One emotion about which adult codependents are particularly unaware is their intense anger over their childhood losses. Rage is probably a more accurate term. Even when the emotional deficit was unavoidable or unintentional—as in the case of a parent's death or extended illness—the loss inevitably resulted in the child's deep, deep anger. Because of their temperament or the emotional environment of the home, those children may have been forbidden or unable to verbalize their rage and disappointment, but that doesn't mean it didn't exist. Even as adults they may be out of touch with their feelings, but the anger, if it hasn't been processed, is still there.

It has been said that the "dialectic of anger . . . is that when it is felt, it disappears, when it is not felt, it remains waiting to be felt."[6] Much of what unconsciously motivates the choices of adult survivors of childhood abuse or abandonment is the rage they were never allowed to feel or express as children. Often the anger experienced in their contemporary relationships is really a displaced anger from an earlier event or situation. A woman sexually abused by her athletic older brother might hate her husband for his interest in Monday night football; a man abandoned by his mother might distrust and verbally abuse his wife; a child homosexually abused by a teacher might grow up to hate homosexuals.

Anger that is unacknowledged doesn't go away. It goes underground. And someone always pays.

NECESSITY OF ADAPTATION

Is it any wonder children learn to adapt in order to survive? In the absence of nurturing parents who help their children increasingly transfer their dependency needs to a loving Father-God, neglected or abandoned children learn to depend on themselves and on others in terribly wrong ways. Soul wounds do not heal if they are ignored. They continue to shape and govern our emotions, our self-images, and our ways of interacting in relationships, long beyond the childhood in which they were received. It is not uncommon for codependents to suddenly wonder what's going on when something happens and their reaction is out of proportion to the surface significance of the incident. Perhaps they are living in a different time zone, thrown back emotionally into a childhood situation they felt unable to handle then and thus feel unable to handle as adults as well. The responses codependents use to manage their lives and relationships as adults have been conditioned by the ways they adapted to the deprivations in their childhoods.

SUMMING UP

This chapter began with an affirmation of our God-given longings for connectedness and impact that begin with our relationships with our parents. These longings were imperfectly met for all of us because all parents are imperfect. For some the loss of adequate parenting was more profound than for others. But we all suffer some degree of woundedness through childhood neglect, abuse, or abandonment. Thus a sketch of the first stages in the development of codependency might look something like this:

Development of Codependency
Longings (for intimacy/impact)
↘
Losses (from parental neglect/abuse)

The next chapter will deal with the formation of self-protective ego facades—adaptation strategies codependents use to emotionally survive their past and present losses because of their unmet longings for intimacy and impact.

QUESTIONS FOR BUILDING COMMUNITY

1. What is the importance of affirming our longings?
2. From John Bradshaw's list of ways parents abandon their children (see pages 86-87), describe one that fits your own experience or the experience of someone you know well.
3. Explain how role reversal is damaging to both parent and child.
4. Tell why you think it is or is not necessary for personal healing that we acknowledge the woundedness of our past.
5. What, if anything, might you do if you realized you'd "lost" your childhood by growing up too fast?

6. What might be a healthy way to help a child deal with his or her anger over losing a parent to sickness or death? To an addiction, compulsion, or codependency?

7. What would be some biblical ways for an adult to deal with repressed or unacknowledged anger from his or her childhood?

8. How would you respond to a Christian who insists, "Don't bring up your parents' sins against you; just get on with obeying God in the present"?

NOTES

1. John Bradshaw, *Bradshaw On: The Family* (Deerfield Beach, FL: Health Communications, Inc., 1988), page 3.

2. Melody Beattie, *Beyond Codependency* (San Francisco, CA: Harper & Row, Publishers, 1989), page 122.

3. Richard Grevengoed, *TODAY, The Family Altar*, a bimonthly devotional guide (Palos Heights, IL: The Back to God Hour), June 13, 1990.

4. Ron Ross, *When I Grow Up . . . I Want To Be an Adult* (San Diego, CA: Recovery Publications, Inc., 1990), page xi.

5. Bradshaw, page 2.

6. Arthur Janov, as quoted by Sandra Simpson LeSourd in *The Compulsive Woman* (Old Tappan, NJ: Fleming H. Revell Company, 1987), page 152.

9

SELF-PROTECTIVE PRETENSE

č

Since one's inner self is flawed by shame, the experience
of self is painful. To compensate, one develops
a false self *in order to survive.*
JOHN BRADSHAW
Bradshaw On: The Family

Consider the dilemma of Randy, a young boy of eleven. He is bright, mildly dyslexic, athletic, rather shy. His parents separated when he was seven; his mother, raised in a restrictively religious home by an aging great-aunt, had run off with another man after her husband, Randy's father, had beaten her "for the last time" (as she tells it). When she finally returned, Randy's father left town; they haven't seen him since.

Randy was also battered physically and verbally by his father, whose raging temper and out-of-control behavior intensified during his frequent drinking episodes. The child was beaten for not understanding his homework, for not waiting patiently outside the bar while his father got drunk, for not being polite to the neighbors, for not anticipating and meeting all of his father's expectations. The abuse left Randy angry, fearful, guilt-ridden, and deeply lonely. Hungry for affection and shamed for being what normal boys are, Randy learned early it wasn't safe being Randy. He would have to become someone else to avoid future abandonment and abuse.

A starving man need not be told to search for food; he instinctively does so. Similarly, a child deprived of parental affection and connectedness naturally seeks a way to either stifle his longings or get them met any way he can. Randy believed himself unlovable because of his parents' abandonment and abuse, so he covered up the precious child he was (with his own unique personality and true feelings) behind a facade of indifference and eventually rebellion. If he'd been able to conceptualize what he was unconsciously doing, he might have explained that this was his way of compensating for his emotional losses from unmet longings for acceptance and parental nurturing.

By age eleven Randy had already learned to hide his real self behind layers of codependent behavior. He experienced self-forfeiture, a sense of being controlled by others with no boundaries regarding his physical or emotional self. He was filled with self-contempt, a low view of his worth and ability because of his parents' abandonment and battering. Children believe what they're told, and Randy was convinced he was worthless. Yet there was also a determined self-aggrandizement in this young boy, a commitment to control his world and the people in it by manipulating the uncles and aunts who took responsibility for him when his parents were both gone. Randy also developed an almost cocky self-sufficiency, taking an extensive paper route at age eight so he wouldn't have to depend on anyone for spending money. And of course he was expert at self-deception, refusing to believe things were as bad as they were and even bragging to himself that he could whip anyone because no kid could hurt him as much as his dad did. Unconsciously and of necessity, Randy learned to survive by becoming something other than the carefree, spontaneous, loved, disciplined, precious eleven-year-old he wanted to be and ought to have been.

FALSE SELVES

Children growing up in dysfunctional homes frequently learn to create a self that can survive the trauma of neglect or abuse. Adult children of alcoholics, for example, adopt distinct and predictable roles to cope with their chaotic family life. Referring to these roles, Drs. Hemfelt, Minirth, and Meier wrote, "All families develop [roles] to a mild extent—the hero, the scapegoat, the lost child, the mascot, the enabler. For persons in a dysfunctional family situation, though, the roles become a coping mechanism, . . . rigid, mindless patterns of behavior easily visible to those outside the family, unrecognized by those within."[1] The roles become masks codependents hide behind for several reasons.

The primary reason a child adopts a role is to please (or appease) his parents. Being himself hasn't worked, so he tries another tack. Dr. Timmen Cermak, a psychiatrist known for his work with children of alcoholics, explained: "If you are a codependent, you please other people because you believe that no one would choose to be with you unless you are serving them. You constantly feel you must earn their love, and you neglect your own needs because you do not feel that you are worthy enough to deserve to have your own needs met."[2] An abused child believes some other kind of child would get the approval or kindness he longs for but hasn't received. So he works to become that other kind of child, hoping to earn the right to be loved. Randy was abandoned, not cherished; battered, not protected; demeaned, not affirmed. But perhaps (his unconscious mind postulated) he might get what he longed for if he were good enough, industrious enough, helpful enough, strong enough. It was worth a try. And if that didn't work, he could rebel, acting out his anger to perversely justify his parents' treatment of him as worthless.

Another reason for constructing a personality facade is to cope with the pain and anger the child feels but dares not acknowledge, even to himself. "The creation of an unreal and false self is often the price of emotional survival, for there is no other way to bear the mental pain of rejection," declared David Seamands.[3] Randy may be raging on the inside, but to stay safe from his father he'd better not rage on the outside. Being "nice" keeps him out of pain better than being "real," so that's what Randy has become, though his camouflaged belligerence occasionally explodes despite his best efforts to control it. Randy will probably grow up angry with the world, yet committed to never making waves with *anyone*, even if he has to sacrifice his emotional integrity in the process. Other abused children may do penance, make jokes, run away, hurt another child (or a pet)—anything that works to muffle or diffuse their inner terror and anger.

Roles are not thoughtfully evaluated and deliberately chosen, like picking a Halloween mask from the toy store shelf. Abused, neglected children just become whatever "works" to help them survive. David Seamands has said, "It is not as if a child consciously decides to become a different person. The decision happens deep in the personality, below the level of awareness."[4] But once the "decision" is made, the child will inevitably develop and carry his ego facade into all adult relationships.

MISPLACED DEPENDENCIES

What is especially sad about children like Randy is that they turn to all the wrong sources for getting their dependency needs met. Instead of being nurtured and gradually taught to transfer their dependency to God and trustworthy others, countless children grow up uncherished and turn to destructive sources for filling the nurturing void. Some choose mood-altering substances to dull the pain, becoming dependent on alcohol or drugs. Others develop compulsions like gambling, shopping, overeating, working, and so on, to somehow try to make them feel good for a time. Many become trapped in relational bondages like codependency, where the seductive hope of "fixing" someone so he or she will finally come through for the codependent drives all concerned to despair and fury. Humanly, those false dependencies—addictions, compulsions, codependency—seem so much more reasonable than depending on God. After all, God didn't "come through" to protect the child from the pain in his world. At least false dependencies are within his control and can be relied upon to provide predictable, if temporary, relief.

Developing false selves and misplaced dependencies does dull the unrelenting pain of the loss of parental connectedness, however. In a culture accustomed to instant relief for every ailment, the substances, habits, and relationships that keep emotional pain at arm's length and help us "make it through the night" work well to medicate our unhappiness.

Wrong dependencies also keep us in control of our lives, or at least they afford the illusion of control. We are determined to prevent a repeat of earlier losses, to never be hurt again. Though our layers of addiction or codependency are discouragingly poor preventatives of future pain, we cling doggedly to them all the same.

Moreover, despite our fear of repeating past losses, we nevertheless unconsciously restage our past (through patterns and relationships that replicate our families of origin), hoping to change that past and fix what went wrong. The repetition compulsion in codependents is fueled by the insatiable need to "correct the original problem, cure the original pain."[5] Our wrong dependencies are meant not only to keep us in charge of our present but also to reconstruct our past with happier endings.

THE BONDAGE OF PRETENSE

One problem with our self-protective false selves and misplaced dependencies is that our masks become our prisons. We become slaves to our facades, and as the false self settles into place, the real person within becomes more and more unsubstantial. How sad to lose one's self, "the self God intended you to be—imperishable, indestructible, and of eternal value in His sight. . . . Alienation from the true self is a terrible price to pay [for emotional survival], and a tragic waste of personhood."[6]

Besides, our wrong dependencies don't "work." They don't get us what we long for and were created to enjoy. We want to be accepted for who we are, but our self-made dungeons keep us from even knowing who we are. We desire the freedom to be authentic and carefree, but we end up bound to others' expectations of who we should be—expectations we ourselves helped to create. Living a lie, being someone we're really not, never deeply satisfies. However attractive the polished exterior of our lives, we never stop longing for someone to open the door of our prison and simply love the disheveled, imperfect inmate of our soul the way a mother embraces her play-soiled child.

From behind the bars of our self-protective pretense we cannot offer freedom and love to anyone else, either. If we free them to be themselves, they might let us down. If we love them for who they are, they might not change into who we need them to be for our benefit. *Instead of loving others, we are committed to obligating them to love us.* Our determination is not to give but to get, and the bondage becomes more, not less, constrictive as the years pass.

INSIDIOUSNESS OF THE FALSE SELF

The insidious aspect about the false self is that it seems so right in the mind of the codependent who has created it. Constructed unconsciously during childhood and working well for years to protect him from feeling his deepest pain, the facade feels normal, familiar, legitimate. Recovering codependents moving toward healthier relationships experience profound discomfort and a sense of abnormality about their newfound freedom to be authentic. People return unthinkingly to the familiar, even when it results in pain or anger. Removing a facade doesn't feel like breaking in a pair of new shoes; it feels like wearing them on the wrong feet. It just doesn't feel "right."

But at an even deeper level of destructiveness, our false selves seem not only familiar but also justified. We believe we deserve our deceptions because we've been hurt so badly in the past. Though our prisons keep us from freedom and love, we think God is an ogre for demanding that we love even those who have harmed us—love them enough to abandon our codependent bondage and relate to them in a new way. We love our pretense because it keeps us safe—safe from being hurt, safe from having to risk loving others in the real world, safe from being truly alive.

SINFULNESS OF SELF-PROTECTIVE PRETENSE

If we are ever to emerge from our prisons of codependency, we must admit that, in addition to protecting us, our masks and pretense have also prevented us from trusting God and from appropriately loving others. Our ego facades are not just *unhelpful* in that they are no longer appropriate or don't work to get us what we want. Rather, we must admit that they are *wrong* because we were created to love God and others, and our pretense and self-protection sabotage both. However justified they may have seemed in helping us survive the losses we suffered as children, we must see our adult codependent strategies as contrary to our original and deepest obligations: dependence on God and mutual interdependence with others.

This suggestion that our codependency is more an evidence of our fallenness than our woundedness may elicit a certain level of outrage even for the codependent deeply committed to recovery. Does God really hold us culpable for employing self-protective strategies that seem entirely reasonable in light of the painful circumstances and relationships we have been required to face? Why should we feel obligated to drop our pretense and pursue authenticity and love with God or anyone else? *We have been wounded!* And God allowed it. What does it mean for a wounded heart to trust God and love people?

These questions cannot be easily answered in a few glib sentences. Struggling to sort out the pain we've experienced from the wrong we have done is difficult at best. But we must grapple courageously with these deep questions of the heart, taking into account both God's compassion for our sorrow and His unflinching call for our obedience. As

His redeemed children we are enjoined to love both Him and others, and we must consider how codependency undermines our attempts to do both. Let's begin by examining how our codependency keeps us from mutual interdependence with others.

Blocked from Loving Others

One of the wonderful things about the pre-Fall relationship between Adam and Eve was their utter lack of shame. They were naked but unashamed, totally open and unprotected, physically and personally. What they'd been given by God—their unique personalities, gifts, and talents—they gladly offered to one another, joyously providing for the other's good. They were not nonpersons, enmeshed in each other, but precious and valued individuals devoted to offering love and freedom.

Contrast that with the self-focused characteristics of codependency. Self-forfeiture, self-contempt, self-aggrandizement, self-sufficiency, self-deception—codependents care less about loving others than about compensating for childhood deficits by getting their own needs met. Dysfunctional people who live behind masks are consumed with self-preoccupation not other-centeredness. Their relationships are inward-directed not outward-directed; their giving is designed to assure their getting something in return.

Moreover, codependents cannot give what is essential to love because they haven't learned to receive it themselves: the freedom to allow others to be who they are. Because of their own bondage to self, codependents cannot offer the most precious of gifts—forgiveness and grace—to the imperfect people who occupy their lives. Thus their bondage constitutes a serious failure to love, a failure for which God holds each of us accountable because He loves us enough to confront us with the only path to life: repentance of sin and acceptance of grace that enables us to live and love as Christ did.

Prevented from Trusting God

The deepest failure of codependents who hide their true selves behind layers of pretense is their disobedience to the commandment Jesus declared to be the "first," or most important: that we love and trust God above all else and with our whole heart (i.e., singlemindedly). When we construct false selves behind which to stay safe, the dynamic behind the pretense is a determination to make our lives work our own way, to keep ourselves in charge of our own lives instead of entrusting ourselves to God's care. Even though Christ gave His life for us, we doubt God's love because our lives haven't gone according to plan—*our* plan. We spurn the gospel of grace in favor of maintaining our independence from God. At the heart of codependent living is an arrogant and fear-based refusal to rely solely on God, an unwillingness to rest in His grace, to be satisifed with His provision and to set our hearts on obedience. Codependency is not just unhelpful but dreadfully and crucially wrong.

SUMMING UP

It is understandable that a wounded child like Randy would develop a false self in order to manage his world and survive emotionally, and that those coping strategies would carry over into his adult relationships. But self-protective pretense designed to dull the pain and prevent the repeat of earlier losses is contrary to what God in His love says is good for us: finding our life in Him and spending our energy gratefully loving Him and others. Codependency violates both of God's foremost purposes for our life, encouraging us instead to find fulfillment apart from Him. Thus a summary chart of the development of codependency might look like this:

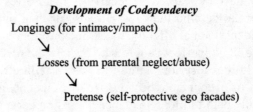

Development of Codependency
Longings (for intimacy/impact)
Losses (from parental neglect/abuse)
Pretense (self-protective ego facades)

The next chapter will examine the mistaken notion that a codependent can find life through pursuing a wrong kind of personal independence from God and others.

QUESTIONS FOR BUILDING COMMUNITY

1. In your own words explain why children in abusive homes develop a "false self."
2. Which event or pattern from your own childhood most encouraged

you to become someone different from who you really were?

3. a. Which "role" best describes the primary way you related within your family of origin?
   - Hero (good kid)
   - Scapegoat (rebel)
   - Lost child (adjuster, avoider)
   - Mascot (comic)

   b. In what way did that role help you? Harm you?

4. Name some specific misplaced dependencies in your own life—i.e., what you depend on (instead of God) to keep you out of pain.

5. Explain why you believe codependency is or is not a sin.

6. How does developing an ego facade violate the command to love and trust God above all?

7. How does developing an ego facade violate the command to love others as ourselves?

8. In a few sentences summarize the chart of how codependency develops: Longings → Losses → Pretense

---

NOTES

1. Robert Hemfelt, Frank Minirth, Paul Meier, *Love Is a Choice* (Nashville, TN: Thomas Nelson Publishers, 1989), page 156.
2. Timmen L. Cermak, *A Time to Heal* (Los Angeles, CA: Jeremy P. Tarcher, Inc., 1988), page 117.
3. David A. Seamands, *Healing Grace* (Wheaton, IL: Scripture Press Publications, 1988), page 99.
4. Seamands, page 97.
5. Hemfelt, Minirth, and Meier, page 70.
6. Seamands, pages 92, 99.

10

AUTONOMOUS INDEPENDENCE

❦

Self-reliance is quite contrary to grace;
. . . extreme self-reliance makes us try
to be our own saviors and sustainers.
DAVID A. SEAMANDS
Healing Grace

When Jesus repeated in Luke 12 what the Old Testament had taught—namely, that man's chief end was to enjoy glad fellowship with God and to love others wholeheartedly—He was describing His own life. Jesus, the perfect Man, modeled truly healthy human living in His own intimate relationship with His Father and in the radical other-centeredness of His relationships with the people in His sphere of influence. Jesus shows us what man's redeemed nature looks like when it is free from self-preoccupation and instead is connected in healthy ways to God and other people.

Codependency violates both principles of our humanness: Our self-sufficiency sabotages our trust in God, and our self-centeredness keeps us from loving others. If we are to become what we are meant to be, we must be healed from the bondage of our codependency. How can we be freed to move from codependent bondage to appropriate bonding with God and others?

Before we deal with a positive answer to that question, let's examine a popular but erroneous "solution" for codependency, a "solution" that, in fact, actually undergirds the problem itself—the development of one's individual autonomy or antidependence.

SPIRIT OF AUTONOMY

Contemporary culture is intoxicated with the heady wine of independence. We write editorials, sing songs, wage verbal battles, and argue court cases over the notion of personal autonomy and individual "rights." We are enjoined to become independent—politically, financially, ethically, religiously, and relationally. "Do your own thing." "Be your own person." "Become self-actualized." "Demand your rights." "Look out for number one."

It's true that God intended that we enjoy freedom to make choices and to live with the consequences of those choices. God also meant for children to grow from total dependency on their parents into independent adults who take responsibility for their choices and consequences. But independence too often means autonomy, which has an altogether different connotation. God never urged people to become autonomous—to govern themselves without His ultimate authority and to determine their own destiny.

Personal autonomy implies that a person can get along just fine without depending on God and/or on other people. Pia Mellody described this antidependence in this way: "I am able to acknowledge to myself that I have needs and wants, but I try to meet them myself and am unable to accept help or guidance from anyone else. I'd rather go without the thing needed or wanted than be vulnerable and ask for help."[1]

Many recovering codependents I know are determined to make it on their own, to stay in control or to regain control over their own lives without having to ask anyone for help. Having been badly damaged, they've decided, "Never again. I'll only enter relationships where I'm in charge." The kind of independence to which they aspire is really anti-God and anti-love. It is a fist thrust toward God that says, "I can and will make my life work on my own!"

This undergirding dynamic of antidependence is evident in the life of King Saul. His codependent characteristics (see chapter 3 for details) cannot simply be attributed to inadequate nurturing or a loss of self. He didn't just need a Twelve-Step program or one-on-one counseling sessions to correct the destructive course on which he was heading. There were deeper heart issues that needed to be addressed.

God, through the prophet Samuel, put His finger on Saul's spiritual pulse and confronted him with this challenge:

To obey is better than sacrifice,
　　and to heed is better than the fat of rams.
For rebellion is like the sin of divination,
　　and arrogance like the evil of idolatry.
　　　　(1 Samuel 15:22-23)

It would not have been enough for Saul to address his "approval junkie" mentality by learning to accept criticism without caving in, not even to realize that his weakness did harm and thus was unloving toward other people. Deep in the heart of Saul was a fist raised against God, a spirit of rebellion and arrogance that stated (through his actions): I am a better judge of what is right in this situation than God is; therefore, I more than He deserve to call the shots. Saul worshiped at the shrine of his own self-sufficiency, and God judged his antidependence by raising up King David to redeem His people.

Can we, any less than Saul, deal with our codependency without looking more closely into the deeper issues of rebellion and arrogance in our souls—the idolatry that lurks in us as surely as it did in him? Important as it is to face our woundedness, isn't our ultimate dilemma, like Saul's, more related to our sin than our pain? Can we hope for freedom from the bondage of codependency without looking to the Redeemer prefigured by David, the only One who can save us not just from our codependency but also from the fierce independence from God that undergirds it?

It seems to me essential to examine our determined and ungodly spirit of autonomy if we're to experience deep change. That spirit might be defined this way:

Autonomous independence is a self-sufficient way of life in which a person attempts to self-generate acceptance, forgiveness, and empowerment apart from God, resulting in spiritual rebellion, a distorted view of self, and problems with intimacy.

Let's take a closer look at the definition.

SELF-SUFFICIENCY *VERSUS* LIFE

Autonomous independence is rooted in sinful self-sufficiency. In contrast to enmeshment, self-sufficiency might be viewed as a desirable alternative to a codependent's loss of personhood. In some ways self-sufficiency has a flavor of appropriate responsibility, the idea of young adults, for example, standing on their own two feet and not needing their parents in the same old way.

However, when we look to Scripture to learn how to live in relationships, we don't read about self-sufficiency or autonomy. What we find instead is God's warning against trusting in ourselves. One proverb straightforwardly declares, "He who trusts in himself is a fool" (Proverbs 28:26). Others build on the same idea:

> Trust in the LORD with all your heart
> > and lean not on your own understanding;
> in all your ways acknowledge him,
> > and he will make your paths straight.
> Do not be wise in your own eyes;
> > fear the LORD and shun evil. (Proverbs 3:5-7)

The psalmist issues a dire warning to those who think they ought to depend only on themselves:

> This is the fate of those who trust in themselves,
> > and of their followers, who approve their sayings.
> Like sheep they are destined for the grave,
> > and death will feed on them. (Psalm 49:13-14)

Autonomous independence in our relationships opens us not to life but to self-destruction and foolishness. It is God-dependence we were designed for, and when we become our own strength, spurning the strength God offers, we become gods and goddesses unto ourselves.

ATTEMPTS TO SELF-GENERATE ACCEPTANCE

Recovering codependents who pursue autonomy try to self-generate acceptance, forgiveness, and empowerment. Determined never to be let down again, they refuse to look to other people or even to God for meeting the deep longings of the heart. The assumption is that only we can truly love and provide for ourselves, so it's foolish to depend on anyone else.

Self-generating the meeting of one's own needs flows from the false notion that the opposite of external referenting (having one's value determined by others) is internal referenting (determining one's worth according to one's own self-approval). Surely it's foolish to bet our emotional portfolio on the likelihood that someone will be able to love us without ever disappointing us. No such human being exists. Codependents held hostage to other people's opinions, moods, and behaviors are right to stop referenting their worth according to others.

But there's no wisdom in trading one kind of slavery for another. We can't depend on our *own* opinion of ourselves, either. We're too flawed to generate our own affirmation; our mood shifts, personal failures, and ingrained negative self-evaluations make us unlikely candidates for reliable self-worth. I don't always like myself, often with good reason. I can't always forgive myself, I'm not always lovable, and my own self-esteem is fickle, at best. On the other hand, I also tend to view myself as better than I really am, justifying my flaws and ignoring my deep failure to love. I need something beyond other people's opinion of me, *and* beyond my own opinion of myself, to use as a reference point for my sense of self-worth.

One reason it's impossible to self-generate approval is that some things are not subject to our own will. Timmen Cermak said, for example,

> Willpower has virtually no ability to control our feelings and
> motivations. . . . Your feelings and motivations are dictated to
> your conscious mind from deep within yourself, from regions of
> your mind that reach back into the past and beyond your ability
> to control what emerges. . . . What we *can* control by force of
> will is whether or not we pay attention to our feelings.[2]

If we cannot control our deepest emotions or motivations but can only learn to listen to them, then we cannot simply take ourselves in hand and convince ourselves of our own worth when for years we've believed ourselves worthless and deserving of punishment. Something from outside ourselves must enter our deepest parts to make changes we cannot make for ourselves.

We need Someone who will never change or waver in His valuing of us or in His commitment to our well-being. No one will do but God Himself.

I cannot self-generate acceptance, but I can find it in God. An eminently reasonable alternative to external referenting or internal referenting is the utter reliability of God-referenting—i.e., defining my worth based on how God sees me. The concept is crucial and will be dealt with in greater detail in coming chapters.

SPIRITUAL REBELLION

One result of a codependent's attempts at recovery through self-generating acceptance, forgiveness, and empowerment is spiritual rebellion—i.e., the refusal to trust God instead of self. People who detach emotionally from God and who never reattach remain spiritually adrift. Cut off from an ongoing experience of communion with God, who is both transcendent (external to us, a reality outside ourselves) and immanent (close to us, the Holy Spirit living within us), they cannot know true Life.

There may be many factors at work in a codependent who refuses to look to God for acceptance, forgiveness, and empowerment. But at the deepest levels of the human soul the reason for our spiritual rebellion is our anger against God. We have expectations of what He should do (or should have done) for us, and we are enraged that He isn't doing it (or didn't do it) in the way or at the time we thought was right.

A recent "Calvin and Hobbes" cartoon episode expresses it well. Calvin is lying on the ground in a heap after being knocked off his swing by Moe, the school bully. Scowling darkly, Calvin declares, "It's hard to be religious when certain people are never incinerated by bolts of lightning."[3]

He's right. It *is* hard to be religious—i.e., to trust in God's goodness and power—when we weren't (or aren't) protected or when those who hurt us weren't (or aren't) punished. Our rage against God, though often not acknowledged (who among us dares to rage openly at an all-powerful God?), lies at the root of our codependent strategies for managing our own lives apart from Him. At some deep level we are doggedly committed to pursuing both safety and autonomy from Him in our scrambling after happiness.

Though we find it sometimes impossible to acknowledge the anger present in our souls, there are sure signs it exists nevertheless. A recent entry I recorded in my journal reads:

> My anger against God doesn't feel like I thought it would. I thought I'd feel deep rage and an overwhelming desire to hurt Him. Instead I find just a deep complaint, a nagging self-pity, a free-floating dissatisfaction with life and relationships, a quiet conviction that I deserve something better, a profound absence of genuine gratitude for God's gifts, a deep belief that I don't need a Savior (I've done quite well at living the Christian life without much help from God or anyone else), and an appalling lack of love for or inner connectedness with God. That angry arrogance shrouds my soul and I am helpless to remove it. I cannot will it away or learn one more thing that will dissolve it. If God does not break in, I am undone. I can only ask—petition—beg for grace . . . and at the same time wonder whether I even want or need it. How profound my rage must be! Deep within is a core of hardness and self-sufficiency, an inner stronghold of resistance to grace that frustrates me as surely as it must grieve the Father. Whatever it is, I love its safety more than I want God right now.

My own recurring antidependence flows from my disappointment with God and my unwillingness to trust Him again. I'd rather depend on myself because in my heart's dark corners I think I'm more trustworthy than He. I know better. Scripture has told me what He's like, and I know from experience how sweet His love and presence can be. Yet I also know from experience the distancing from Him that can come from my stubborn self-sufficiency. During such times (and they are more frequent than I like to admit) I am spiritually out of sync, and my worship becomes mere ritual, formality without substance, frighteningly like Paul's description of "having a form of godliness but denying its power" (2 Timothy 3:5). Those demoralizing pockets of spiritual sterility haunt me because I know I was built for something better—a vital relationship with my loving, heavenly Father—and my autonomy sabotages what my heart longs to have. Thank God He doesn't leave me there. A later chapter will explore a biblical solution to the dilemma of our antidependent spirit toward God.

DISTORTED VIEW OF SELF

Another result of my autonomous spirit is that I "think of [myself] more highly than [I] ought" (Romans 12:3). I fancy myself self-sufficient, thinking I have more power over my life than I really do. A friend called me the other day to complain about the circumstances of her life: her mother's precarious health, the uncertainty of her job, her failure to get into the college class she wanted, the loss of a romantic relationship she had depended on. She had a rather long list of disappointments. I understood. I was experiencing some of the same frustrations myself that day. And codependent that I am, my first reaction was to try to help her find solutions to her problems, to fix what was wrong in her life. There's nothing wrong with trying to solve our own problems or suggesting ways others can solve theirs. But my inclination to control the whole world flows from my distorted view of myself as far more powerful than I really am.

Another error common to recovering codependents is their determination to establish "boundaries" so they won't be victimized anymore. Surely, it's right to refuse to be used by others; loving others properly will put an unequivocal halt to the codependent's self-abuse. But when a person's priority in life is self-protection, that person hasn't yet realized the purpose God intended for relationships: a free willingness to offer ourselves to others out of overflow, not deficit. Boundary-setting for the sake of self-protection ignores God's command to move toward others in genuine love, even though it will mean uncomfortable change and messy relationships. Recovering codependents too easily rush out of even committed relationships like marriage in order to find safety from being hurt again.

Our boundaries (i.e., our limits regarding what others do to and with us physically and emotionally) must be set, not just by what feels good to us but also by what is good for the other person's spiritual welfare. When we genuinely love, we don't allow others to harm or abuse us—not just because we don't like it but also because it fails to invite the perpetrators to repentance and change. They may dislike the limits we set in love, but we can be genuinely unselfish in refusing to be victimized.

Another underlying self-image distortion characterizing autonomy is that codependents remain self-preoccupied. Their attention is not directed toward God or others but toward themselves. They are consumed with looking good, even in recovery. When I began to abandon my codependency, I wanted to "recover right" and was terrified of making a mistake. It was the same old codependency clothed in new "recovery" garments—my old willpower trying to change myself in the right way at the right time with no mess-ups along the way. It was humiliating to acknowledge that even in being freed from codependency I was preoccupied with *me* and no one else. In fact, my process often bulldozed forward at others' expense. In my hurry to "get well" I often neglected everyone else's needs or feelings. Ask my family and friends. The "new" me may have looked less codependent, but I certainly wasn't a better lover.

PROBLEMS WITH INTIMACY

It's not surprising that autonomous independence is counterproductive to intimacy. Instead of alleviating demandingness, autonomy makes even more demands—that the other "be there" for us because we've discovered that's what we need and deserve. We may stop being subtle and simply tell others just what they should do for us. I went from never directly asking Bill for anything (and being quietly enraged that he hadn't read my mind) to demanding outright that he do things for me, then verbally lashing out at him when he didn't. I treated my friends the same way. It was, to say the least, a tumultuous time for everyone concerned. If I had stopped at the point of getting in touch with and expressing my anger (and many do stop there), I would have short-circuited my recovery. Anger and demandingness are stops along the way toward facing our deeper issues, but they are not the final destination of the healing codependent.

We were created for healthy dependence on God and others, and autonomous independence sabotages both. When we ignore or reject our legitimate and appropriate need for others, we violate the call of our redeemed nature, which is to give to and receive love from others out of the abundance of love God has shown us. God's directive to love is not negated because other people fail to love us. That directive—along with the command that we worship God above all else—is still the reason we're here on earth.

The recovering codependent's spirit of autonomy undermines genuine intimacy with the important people in his or her life. Acceptance, forgiveness, and the freedom to be authentic are essential to intimate relationships, and autonomous independence goes contrary to all three because it pushes the codependent into demandingness and self-preoccupation.

SUMMING UP

Because we were created with the need, capability, and command to bond with others, self-sufficient autonomy violates our very nature as human beings. Trying to self-generate acceptance, forgiveness, and empowerment keeps us from finding our life in God, from enjoying a balanced view of ourselves, and from genuinely bonding with others. On our diagram of the development of codependency, the spirit of autonomy is not part of the upward movement toward recovery from codependency but the downward negative end of a self-centered way of life. It might look like this:

Development of Codependency

Longings (for intimacy/impact)

↘

Losses (from parental neglect/abuse)

↘

Pretense (self-protective ego facades)

↘

Autonomy (refusal to trust or need)

What makes the codependent's autonomy most insidious is that the refusal to trust or need violates the very thing most necessary for recovery. Honestly admitting helplessness over one's unhealthy attachment to abusive relationships is the first step in a codependent's spiritual journey into life.

For decades men, women, and children have started on the road to recovery from addiction by taking the first step of the Alcoholics Anonymous Twelve-Step recovery program, acknowledging: *"We admitted we were powerless over alcohol* [or gambling or overeating or codependency]—*that our lives had become unmanageable."* Our helplessness, the acknowledged failure of our willpower to hold our lives together in the face of our overwhelming addiction, is the door to hope because it opens us up to the help we need but cannot give ourselves. Autonomous independence is the antithesis of acknowledged need; it sabotages from the very start our long-term recovery from codependency.

The next section will outline the ingredients necessary for genuine and long-lasting recovery—freedom from the bondage of codependent relationships and a healthy bonding (or rebonding) with God and others.

QUESTIONS FOR BUILDING COMMUNITY

---

1. Why does Scripture speak out against autonomy or self-sufficiency? What does it command instead?
2. How would you describe the difference between "life" and "a way of life"?
3. How is self-generating acceptance similar to the image of pulling oneself up by one's own bootstraps?
4. In what ways did Jesus "set boundaries"? How did it relate to His loving?
5. Are you angry at God? Why, or why not?
6. What are some ways a person might experience anger and/or anti-dependence toward God?
7. Name some specific ways autonomous independence interferes with genuine intimacy in your life or in the life of someone you know well.
8. How would you define appropriate dependence on God and others? Why are both important for a recovering codependent?

NOTES

1. Pia Mellody, Andrea Wells Miller, J. Keith Miller, *Facing Codependence* (San Francisco, CA: Harper & Row, Publishers, 1989), page 29.
2. Timmen L. Cermak, *A Time to Heal* (Los Angeles, CA: Jeremy P. Tarcher, Inc., 1988), page 125.
3. Calvin and Hobbes copyright 1990 Universal Press Syndicate. Reprinted with permission. All rights reserved.

PART THREE

WHAT IS THE ROUTE TO BONDING?

11

THE HEALING OF GRIEF

❧

Deep grieving purges. If it is not done, and the list
[of wrongs] is not thereby relegated to the past, the losses
become part of the cycle again, entering at the pain spot.
ROBERT HEMFELT, FRANK MINIRTH, PAUL MEIER
Love Is a Choice

If autonomous independence is the antithesis of recovery from code-pendency, then what is a biblical alternative? We must revoke our destructive and painful styles of relating, but godly relationships won't feel as good nor as safe as self-sufficiency. The road to biblical healing winds through grief and pain, uncertainty and risk, repentance and confession, unpredictability and danger. It is the narrow path Jesus beckons us to walk, leading us into the terror of grace and the humility of abject dependence on God. Those who choose it will seem crazy, sometimes even to themselves.

Why renounce both codependence and antidependence? Why choose God's dangerous journey into grace? In a word, the reason is *life*. God invites us into pain because loving always costs us pain. He offers us danger because fighting evil is never safe. He promises us persecution because God's people—including His beloved Son—have always been misunderstood and opposed. Resting in Jesus is infinitely harder than accomplishing our own agendas. Trusting grace feels more demeaning than earning our salvation. Coming alive to hope is more painful and cruel than being dead to our emotions. But it is life. And once we've tasted being alive, we can't go back to being dead. Aliveness in God is addictive.

MOVING INTO GRIEF

The first stage of coming alive involves the opposite of what we expect; it involves an awakening into grief. Codependents are expert at numbing their souls. Thawing frozen emotions is like warming frostbitten fingers: It hurts. But it's better than gangrene and amputation.

Three kinds of grief are necessary: grief over our losses (past and present disappointments in relationships); grief over our self-protective pretenses (ego facades designed to shield us from our losses); and grief over our autonomous independence (self-sufficient determination to make our lives work apart from God). Let's explore the three kinds of grieving.

GRIEVING LOSSES

Codependents begin the grieving process by admitting the damage done to them, particularly in childhood. What others did or failed to do caused them harm, and recovering codependents must acknowledge the disappointment of their early losses of nurturing and connectedness.

Someone has compared our having been wounded by our parents to the experience of a child whose parents backed the car out of the garage and ran over his foot. They didn't *intend* to run over his foot, but that doesn't mean the child wasn't hurt. Childhood losses are real, even when unintended, even when one's parents did the best they could, given their own woundedness. Alice Miller once said, "When you were young, you needed something you did not receive, and you will never receive it. And the proper attitude is mourning . . . not blame."[1] *We cannot be healed of the wounds we won't acknowledge.*

The purpose of facing our pain is twofold. First, we can't be authentic unless we're honest about the emotional realities of our lives. If we won't face our pain, we'll go on barricading ourselves behind pretense and never achieve openness—an essential element in genuine intimacy.

Second, if we won't face our losses, we can't move toward forgiveness and restoration. Grief opens the door to freedom from past and present damage, with all its hidden angers and subconscious resentments. David Seamands pointed out that Joseph, a victim of abuse at the hands of his brothers, didn't excuse their perversity nor minimize the impact of their sin, but clearly confronted them with the truth. "You intended to harm me," he told them (Genesis 50:20). *Then* he forgave them and "spoke kindly to them" (verse 21). As Seamands pointed out, "We can't really forgive [those who have sinned against us] until we admit how much they've hurt us, and then face how we feel toward them. . . . Many people today mistakenly think that forgiveness means to overlook the evils done against them; they feel they are being sweet, loving Christians. Actually, this is an exercise in unreality which keeps out the power of grace."[2] Our honest grieving over our disappointments opens us to the grace we need from God, which we can then offer to others.

Past pain can sometimes be best entered across the threshold of present relational pain. What is harmful in present relationships likely mirrors what happened in past relationships. By paying attention to how we feel now when we're abused, dismissed, or rejected, we can enter how we felt as children when those things happened to us. When the pain (present or past) comes, we must choose to let it in.

In fact, we must grieve our present losses as well as our past disappointments, especially those related to the addiction or compulsion of those close to us. What others are doing to abuse us and what we continue doing as codependents cause enormous damage, and we must mourn our irretrievable opportunities to do one another good instead of harm.

The grieving will open us to unwelcome emotions like anger and sadness. Especially at first there may be a welling up of resentment and a desire to alienate ourselves from those who hurt us. This natural reaction ought not to be ignored or repressed, but simply felt. Denial has probably kept these important emotions at bay for years, and by the time they are acknowledged, they are long overdue. Our call is not to act on those negative emotions—by expressing our rage or abandoning relationships, for example—but to be willing to feel them. Grief need not end in resentment or alienation, though it often begins or pauses there on the way to healing.

GRIEVING SELF-PROTECTIVE PRETENSE

If we're to heal deeply and embrace a godly alternative to codependency, we must grieve our pretense as well as our losses. The grief is not the same.

Children resort to pretense in order to survive. They adopt false selves so they can manipulate their world and stay alive emotionally. In response to specific experiences of abuse or neglect and according to their individual temperaments, they engage in self-protective strategies for staying safe instead of learning to pursue other-centered love. As adults, those same children cling to their ego facades in a desperate attempt to undo the trauma or restage their childhood experiences with happier endings. The wounded become the wounders.

However, our past woundedness is no excuse for our present pretense. Even if we'd had perfect parents, we'd have developed ego facades to remain independent from God and safe from other people. No one escapes the effect of the Fall. We're all flawed lovers, and it's not just our parents' fault. Childhood damage doesn't justify self-protective love failures. Our pretense does great harm to ourselves and to others, and we must face and grieve that damage. Scripture calls that kind of grief *repentance*.

Damage to Self

Codependent strategies intended to protect the codependent actually result in greater self-harm. Self-forfeiture, for example, is counter-productive to the mutuality of relationship we deeply desire. A marionette has nothing to offer but compliance, and compliance isn't intimacy. When we act like pawns in someone else's chess game, we destroy God's image in us, disenfranchising ourselves from making our own choices. Our chosen self-forfeiture is a self-protective strategy we must both repent and hold ourselves accountable to change.

We must also repent our self-contempt, our perverse complicity in denigrating God's giftedness in us. When we neglect or hate or shame ourselves, when we deny our value or hold it hostage to the opinion of others, we declare God's Word invalid (that we are precious—Isaiah 43:4) and despise His handiwork. We must grieve (i.e., repent) our chosen loss of self.

Damage to Others

Our ego facades also damage others. Self-aggrandizement and self-sufficiency are particularly harmful because they sabotage what we were all created to enjoy. No relationship can thrive in a control-based environment; we were built for freedom and mutual respect. My attempts to control Bill (telling him how to drive, what to say, how to handle his relationship with Christopher, etc.) emasculated him by the inch. He won't let me get away with it anymore, and rightly so. Isolating myself and playing self-righteous games at church harm my brothers and sisters in Christ. When I martyr myself to look good, I'm using others to stage my own melodrama, seeking applause at their expense. I must repent of the damage my self-protective strategies have caused others.

GRIEVING AUTONOMOUS INDEPENDENCE

The dynamic undergirding of all our codependent strategies is an avid commitment to making life work without God. Our refusal to need God or to enjoy mutual interdependence with others is a grievous offense in God's eyes. Though it seems eminently reasonable for us to light our own path in the emotional blackness caused by past and present losses, God invites us to simply trust Him in the dark and warns us of the dire consequences of *not* trusting Him. Listen to His word through Isaiah the prophet:

> Let him who walks in the dark,
>   who has no light,
> trust in the name of the LORD
>   and rely on his God.
> But now, all you who light fires
>   and provide yourselves with flaming torches,
> go, walk in the light of your fires
>   and of the torches you have set ablaze.
> This is what you shall receive from my hand:
>   You will lie down in torment. (Isaiah 50:10-11)

Does God have strong opinions about our determined self-sufficiency? Lying down in torment seems harsh penalty for what seems so justifiable—i.e., trusting our own resources to make life work. Yet it reveals the heart of God toward His children: *Our greatest good is in trusting Him alone for the resources we need to live rich and meaningful lives.* He hates autonomy because it destroys what we're meant to enjoy—rich fellowship with Him by resting in His grace and provision.

At deep levels of rebellion, autonomy works to keep us safe from

God and to prove we can live without Him. Our codependent strategies are our way to save ourselves without God's help; our niceness, help-fulness, or religiosity act as our "saviors." Wonderful as we may look on the outside, inside we raise quiet fists in defiance against God and His call to find life only in Himself.

Our willingness to confront and repent of our strategies to make life "work" without utter dependence on God will depend ultimately on how we define "life." *What is it for us that makes life worth living?* If "life" for us is deep and growing communion with a God who loves us, repentance and recovery will be difficult but joyfully possible. If, on the other hand, life is found in having, or trying to get, the intimacy and impact we want when and how we want it, we spit on the cross and trample the gospel underfoot. We, the abused, become abusers of the One who died for us.

If we choose to move toward repentance we discover that our scrupulously polished exteriors camouflage deep self-centeredness. We must grieve not only about how bad things were (and are) for us but also about how wonderful we mistakenly thought *we* were all along. God invites us to open our whitewashed tombs and expose the decadence of our lives to the cleansing power of His grace.

HINDRANCES TO REPENTANCE

It's an understatement to say we must grieve (i.e., repent) for what we've done to violate the three great loves we owe: to God, to others, and to self. We have shunned God, rejecting His grace in order to maintain our self-sufficiency. We have failed to love others with the kind of passionate other-centeredness God requires. And we have revictimized ourselves, refusing to believe we're loved with an everlasting love that prompts genuine self-love and grateful obedience.

However, we may have to begin by dealing with what often hinders repentance. First, we must confront our assumption that facing past and present disappointments will result in a total loss of emotional con-trol. Codependents are terrified that entering their sorrow or rage might create an emotional avalanche, sweeping everything, including them-selves, before it in devastation. The risk of that may block repentance, unless we remember that God will never forsake us. We will surely experience some unsettling and even excruciating emotions along the path to change, but God's Spirit will strengthen us for whatever we encounter, and His people can support us along the way.

We also hate admitting fault in a relationship where we've been accustomed to blaming the other person. Bill and I played the blame game during most of our married lives, and one evidence of our increasing relational health is that we can both acknowledge our failure to love in any given moment. All codependents want to believe they're only victims and not agents, but it's liberating to repent—asking for and receiving forgiveness for our wounding of God and others.

BENEFITS OF GRIEVING

Grief has its rewards on all three of our codependent levels—losses, pretense, and autonomy. One benefit of entering the pain of our losses is an experiential knowledge of how we've harmed and disappointed others. Codependents are said to be better at feeling others' pain than at feeling their own. More likely, however, they feel others' pain so that they don't have to feel their own. If they allowed themselves into their own woundedness, they'd know the damage of their own wounding of others. When I bled at Bill's verbal sword-wounds, I was able to feel how my words hurt him. When I realized and experienced my own nurturing losses, I recognized how I'd failed to nurture Christopher.

Grief also engages us as we deal with our ego facades. My initial grief over my self-protection deeply shamed me, and I had to shift from a preoccupation with how I felt (I'm such a lousy lover!) to a painful ownership of how I'd damaged others (my friends hurt because I've withheld my true self from them). In repenting our pretense we must move beyond self-justification (I deserve to protect myself) or revenge (she had it coming) or comparison (I hurt her less than she hurt me) or even the other person's indifference (she doesn't care enough to be hurt by me). We must allow the full impact of our failure to love to hit us as hard as if it had been done to us, to transfer the other person's feelings to ourselves. Entering the other person's pain over our love failure moves us toward the heart of genuine grief for creating a false self that cannot love deeply or authentically.

Most significantly, as I entered the pain of others turning against me, I also felt the Father's pain at my autonomous independence from Him. How amazing that my actions have an impact on the God of the universe! When the Israelites repented after God had punished them for their idolatry, God finally "could bear Israel's misery no longer" (Judges 10:16). The image of God grieving over His people's misery is wondrous to me. Does God weep when I use the gifts He gave me to protect myself instead of to bless others? Does He groan when I insist on trusting myself by permitting abuse? I think we know very little of the wounded heart of God on our behalf.

Yet the Father's heart, though wounded, longs for restoration with His precious children, and it's our repentance that opens us to forgiveness and grace. God never turns from a repentant heart; David declared, "A broken and contrite heart, O God, you will not despise" (Psalm 51:17). Until we have acknowledged and repented of our sin and have tasted God's forgiveness, we can't forgive ourselves or anyone else.

But when we do repent, we find rich comfort in being freed from our guilt. Gerald May said, "The biblical Hebrew word for repentance was *nacham*, 'to be comforted' or 'eased.'"[3] Our grieving in repentance brings us the comfort of being forgiven, the easing of our consciences over our failure to love God, ourselves, and others.

HOW SHOULD WE GRIEVE?

One final word about grief. Children raised on the three rules described by Claudia Black (don't talk, don't trust, don't feel) find it difficult to authentically grieve. They have for so long repressed or ignored their own feelings they think they have no feelings at all. How can codependents learn to grieve?

We learn to grieve our pain by seeing how others—a counselor or close friend or members of a support group—respond with their own grief to the stories we tell about ourselves. I remember the wonder I felt when my counselor cried as I recounted an abusive event in my life. I had not felt the depth of sorrow on my own behalf until someone mirrored it back to me, and I let my pain in at a much deeper level. Over time I'm getting better at owning my true feelings even without someone else's affirmation of how I should feel. I'm learning to cry for myself.

I'm also learning to weep over my sin. Perhaps the best way to enter repentance for our pretense and autonomy is to open our hearts to God's Word to us. Conviction of sin is a function of grace, a work the Holy Spirit does within us at our invitation. I've found Him relentless, even brutal, in responding to such an invitation. Sometimes He works directly through a passage of Scripture or through His own quiet witness to my heart as I "tune in" to the underlying dynamics of a given interaction with a friend or relative. At other times He uses the rebuke of a friend (or even an opponent) to open my eyes to my own love failures. Solomon told us in Proverbs 27:6 that "wounds from a friend can be trusted"; they usher us into conviction and godly sorrow. As I walk through repentance into grace, the precious knowledge that I'm loved as I am and that His grace is sufficient makes me bold to even welcome reproof from God and others. "Where sin increased, grace increased all the more," said the Apostle Paul (Romans 5:20). Thanks be to God!

SUMMING UP

The development of a person's codependency moves more or less predictably through the stages of longings, losses, and pretense. Often a "recovering" codependent will adopt a spirit of autonomy in an attempt to regain a greater sense of control over his or her life.

But genuine recovery from codependency follows a different path. Like the development of codependency, recovery is less a chronological movement than a continuing spiral of repeatedly dealing with life's realities in a new way. The first aspect of the biblical process of recovery from codependency is grief—i.e., sorrow for—one's losses and repentance for one's pretense and autonomy. It might be diagramed this way:

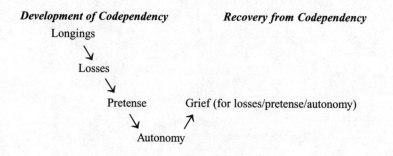

The following chapter will explore a second aspect of recovery: the necessity and wonder of grace.

QUESTIONS FOR BUILDING COMMUNITY

1. What keeps you from facing the pain of your childhood losses of nurturing and intimacy?
2. What prevents you from grieving your disappointments in present relationships?
3. How is your refusal to acknowledge and grieve your losses (past and present) keeping you from loving others well?
4. What is the difference between "niceness" and Christlike love?
5. What would have to happen in order for you to deeply feel how you've damaged others, especially those close to you?
6. What difference would it make in your life if you believed God hurt as much over your autonomous independence from Him as you hurt over the damage done to you?
7. Name some ways in which codependents raise inner fists in rebellion against God.
8. What is the connection between repentance and grace in regard to relationship with God? With those close to us?

NOTES

1. Alice Miller, as quoted by Robert Bly in a televised interview with Bill Moyers, entitled *A Gathering of Men* (New York: Journal Graphics, Inc., 1990), transcript page 12.
2. David A. Seamands, *Healing Grace* (Wheaton, IL: Scripture Press Publications, 1988), page 130.
3. Gerald G. May, *Addiction and Grace* (San Francisco, CA: Harper & Row, Publishers, 1988), page 192, footnote 13.

12

THE WONDER OF GRACE

❦

After many years of pastoral ministry in which it has been
my privilege to counsel people of varying races and cultures,
I have come to a strong conclusion that the last thing
we humans surrender to God is an admission
of our helplessness to save ourselves.
DAVID A. SEAMANDS
Healing Grace

Though grieving our losses, pretense and autonomy is essential to recovery from codependency, it's not enough just to get in touch with our feelings or to realize our sin. Owning our woundedness and recognizing our self-protection doesn't go far enough. What we need is a *solution* to our dilemma of pain and guilt.

In our attempt to satisfy our deepest desires, we attach them to behaviors, things, or people we think can assuage our thirst for intimacy, acceptance, freedom, and forgiveness—things we ultimately desire from God. These attachments (to a substance, an idea, a spouse, a job, etc.) are compulsive and ultimately disillusioning. We are kidnapped by our false attachments, imprisoned by our codependency, and unable to liberate ourselves. As Dr. Gerald May has said, "To be alive is to be addicted, and to be alive and addicted is to stand in need of grace."[1]

In fact, *it is in our very inability to perfect ourselves that our hope appears*, "for it is in failure and helplessness that we can most honestly and completely turn to grace. Grace is our only hope for dealing with addiction."[2] If we are to break free from our bondage to codependency, we must petition for grace. Let's consider what that means.

RECOVERY PROCESS

The Alcoholics Anonymous recovery program includes a list of twelve steps alcoholics take to establish and maintain their sobriety. These steps are both consecutive and cyclical; that is, they are to be taken more or less in sequence, and not only once but continually. "Working the steps" is a lifelong process.

The twelve steps are also used in the recovery process from other compulsions, such as drug abuse, gambling, overeating, workaholism, etc. The remaining chapters of this book will examine these twelve steps in relationship to breaking free from codependency.

The first step in the AA program says, *"We admitted we were powerless over alcohol—that our lives had become unmanageable."* In other words, the alcoholic admitted his addiction was so compulsive as to prevent his will from controlling it. He was powerless to manage his life in the sense that his attachment to alcohol ultimately superseded his every attempt to "straighten up."

This is not an easy admission to make. The tenacity with which addicts cling to their habits is strong evidence of how jealously they guard their "right" to be self-sufficient. "I can quit any time I want to" is the standard defense of every alcoholic, no matter how hopelessly addicted. But no lasting power is available to help them quit the habit until that first step is taken: *the admission of powerlessness*.

For a codependent, the first step might mean acknowledging helplessness over alcohol or another mood-altering substance. He or she must deal with the addiction before dealing with the codependency undergirding it. Melody Beattie, in her book *Codependent No More*, acknowledged, "Not once, but twice in my lifetime, I had tried to do the impossible. I tried to control alcohol. I had battled with alcohol in my own drinking and using days; I went to war again with alcohol when people I loved were using and abusing it."[3] Codependency and substance abuse often go hand in hand.

All codependents, whether addicted themselves or in some way related to someone who is, must take the first step in recovery, admitting they are powerless to control the person or relational habit to which they've attached their desires. Acknowledging our inability to manage our lives through our own resources is excruciating but altogether necessary.

Step Two in the AA program says we *"came to believe that a Power greater than ourselves could restore us to sanity."* When we come to the end of ourselves (which is God's purpose for us all), we realize help must come from a Power greater than we are. In other words, though many in the AA and Al Anon community wouldn't put it this way, we as Christians acknowledge our need for grace. And as my pastor, Steve Brown, said, "Grace operates only in the context of one's acknowledgment there is no option *but* grace."[4] If we face the limits of our humanness by admitting our powerlessness, we're ready for grace from a Power beyond ourselves.

But even as we admit our need for help from God, we must also struggle with the reality that in our deepest hearts we hate to give up our autonomy. We are torn by our ambivalence between longing for intimacy with God while at the same time despising the horror of depending utterly on Him alone. We know we should love Him and sometimes we do. But we're also enraged because He has disappointed us, and we don't want to trust Him again. We even (probably unconsciously) hate Him for demanding that we love others in spite of our having been wounded so badly ourselves.

Even for codependents who are committed to recovery it's not easy to recognize or acknowledge the entrenched outrage in our souls. Ultimately, however, only a heart deeply gripped by the reality of its rebellion against a good and loving God can be open to the miracle of grace. Until we face how wicked that rebellion is in God's eyes, we will continue to live life on our terms, not God's, and our raised fists will keep out the gift of grace God says is our only way to renewed fellowship with Him.

It is an age-old dilemma. King Saul struggled with it and chose death instead of life. Other Old Testament heroes—such as Abraham, Moses, David, and Daniel—struggled and chose life. Many of Jesus' followers, when confronted with His message that His sacrifice was the only way to the Father, deserted Him because the teaching was too hard (John 6:35-66).

Listen to the crucial exchange that followed between Jesus and His twelve most devoted disciples:

Many of his disciples turned away and deserted him. Then Jesus turned to the Twelve and asked, "Are you going too?"

> Simon Peter replied, "Master, to whom shall we go?
> You alone have the words that give eternal life, and we
> believe them and know you are the holy Son of God." (John
> 6:67-69, TLB)

The same exchange must take place between Christ and those of us who want to recover from codependency or any other alternative to the gospel. *To whom shall we go?* Do we know a better way to live than through accepting the grace Christ offers us? Most of us thought we did, but what we've tried hasn't ushered us into anything but emptiness and frustration.

To depend on God or to love others who can hurt us seems utterly unreasonable until we consider the alternative. We have pursued self-protection long enough now to know there is no real life in our strategies. As frightening and painful as it is to repent of and turn from our autonomy, we know there is no other route to experiencing the grace and sufficiency of God.

Sometimes trusting God to preserve the deepest parts of who we are as we abandon our false selves and offer our real self to Him and others feels like an outrageous risk. *But what other option does any of us have if we truly desire Life?* The way may seem treacherous, and it is. Christ gave His life on that path. But His life relinquished became our life eternal. Ultimately, faith in His grand accomplishment is the only thing that will sustain us as we walk as He walked. With the psalmist we can declare with passion, "Whom have I in heaven but you? And earth has nothing I desire besides you. My flesh and my heart may fail, but God is the strength of my heart and my portion forever" (Psalm 73:25-26).

If we are willing to risk moving toward dependence on God and mutual interdependence with others, we will find God's grace available in all of its many facets. Just what "kinds" of grace do we need?

FORGIVING GRACE

Ever since the Fall, mankind's greatest relational need is for forgiveness. We have spurned our dependence on God and violated mutual interdependence, and without forgiveness from God and others we are doomed to perish in our loneliness and rage.

When we consider that codependency is basically self-focused, it becomes clear that our development of a "false self" has kept us from genuinely loving God and others. It has also kept us from appropriately caring for the true or real self. Our pretense and autonomy make all of us legitimately and truly guilty—for failing to love God, self, and others. Our greatest grace imperative is for forgiveness in the face of our rebellion against God through self-sufficiency and our sin against God and others in failing to love. The fact that we think those who have harmed us need forgiveness more than we do is beside the point. Focusing on others' sin will keep us from acknowledging the irrefutable fact that we, too, have failed to love perfectly—and we stand in desperate need of grace.

God's "solution" is not to somehow get us to work harder to achieve what He commands us to do—i.e., love Him and others. Rather, He calls us to admit we have not done and cannot do what He commands—our fallen nature makes it impossible. In the face of that impossibility to be perfect, we are left with the ultimate choice: despair or grace.

It is precisely in the darkness of our utter helplessness that the wonder of God's grace dawns on our souls with its greatest beauty. What we cannot do for ourselves—i.e., earn God's favor by striving to be good—Jesus Christ accomplished for us by paying the penalty of our sin on Calvary and offering us His righteousness in exchange. God's forgiveness of those who put their faith in the substitutionary death of His Son, Jesus, is the essence of the gospel of grace—His light penetrating our darkness and illuminating our only way to the Father.

Grace refers to God's undeserved kindness directed toward those who believe in Jesus. David Seamands defined it as "God's love in action on our behalf, freely giving us His forgiveness, His acceptance, and His favor."[5] God Himself did for us what we could not do for ourselves: He (Jesus) paid the penalty for our sins. The Apostle John promised, "If we confess our sins, he is faithful and just and will forgive us our sins and purify us from all unrighteousness" (1 John 1:9). God's forgiving grace is undeserved, unearned, and unrepayable. The "Power greater than ourselves" has restored us to more than sanity; He has restored us to the fellowship with Himself for which we were created, returning us to our full humanness once again. Those who refuse His grace miss Life.

GRACE FOR LOSSES

Just as recovering codependents must grieve their losses, pretense, and autonomy, they also must receive grace for those same things. Let's first consider grace for our losses.

God offers us codependents a special kind of grace as we deal with our past and present pain in relationships. It is what I call *comforting grace*.

Comforting grace is found in the Father's gracious presence in the midst of our pain. Recovering codependents generally expect that abandoning their destructive habits will reverse the tide of their lives so they'll no longer hurt. What usually happens is the opposite: The pain increases, because now reality settles in without the medicating effect of their former compulsions. Then they cry out to God: "I'm doing what You called me to do. I'm trying to not control and blame others or despise myself anymore. So why aren't things getting better?"

I've been there. I believed if I did my part, God would reward me for being good by improving my circumstances (or my husband or son or parents). I knew the expectation was biblically unwarranted, but in my heart I was counting on it. I was disappointed.

What exactly *does* God promise about our pain? Isaiah, God's prophet to the people of Judah during a difficult time in their history, had powerful words of comfort for them. They would suffer because of their sin, but in the midst of their suffering God would provide something wonderful:

> When you pass through the waters,
>   I will be with you;
> and when you pass through the rivers,
>   they will not sweep over you.
> When you walk through the fire,
>   you will not be burned;
>   the flames will not set you ablaze. . . .
> Do not be afraid, for I am with you. (Isaiah 43:2,5)

The message is clear, if unexpected: In this life you will have trouble and it won't be fun. Isaiah wrote *when*, not *if*, you pass through deep waters and walk through fire, thus preparing God's people for coming trauma. We, too, must expect problems to plague us until we're Home, even though we're precious in God's sight and beloved. To endure our trials we have only one promise: the grace of God's presence. It's not exactly what we wanted; we were counting on relief from pain and a return on our emotional investment in others. Nor does God's presence always seem adequate—unless we consider the alternative. To be abandoned by the Father, as Jesus on our behalf was forsaken by Him on the cross, is the worst possible fate I can imagine. His presence is sweetness and life, His absence despair and death. It is comforting grace to know He's with me in every circumstance and He so identifies with me that He tastes salt when I cry. We are told as much in Psalm 103:13-14:

> As a father has compassion on his children,
>> so the LORD has compassion on those who fear him;
> for he knows how we are formed,
>> he remembers that we are dust.

What comfort to bask in the grace of God's Father-love.

GRACE FOR PRETENSE

A second kind of grace, grace for our pretense, is what I call God's *empowering grace*. God offers us love beyond our own for the unlovable people in our lives. He provides the power to behave in a way consistent with others' good, even when we are deeply hurt ourselves. For recovering codependents this is an essential grace; our strategies for escaping pain in ways that protect us but damage others are impossible to change through our own willpower.

Before His death, Jesus prepared His disciples for the coming of His Spirit, saying, "I will ask the Father, and he will give you another Counselor to be with you forever—the Spirit of truth . . . [who] will be in you" (John 14:16-17). The work of the Holy Spirit in the life of every believer produces inner qualities that break down self-protective ego facades and nourish interdependent relationships. The Apostle Paul defined these as "love, joy, peace, patience, kindness, goodness, faithfulness, gentleness and self-control" (Galatians 5:22-23). There is no resource of willpower or goodness in ourselves from which to draw those attributes. We need God's empowering grace if we are to destroy our pretense by moving toward others with Christlike boldness minus the safety of our masks.

The wonderful thing about grace is that it changes us, sometimes dramatically, sometimes imperceptibly. When we repent our pretense and receive the Father's grace to cover our sin, we are transformed by the transaction. In repentance we sink our roots deep into the fertile ground of grace, and the fruit of God's Spirit buds and matures without our striving or straining. It's only when we refuse grace and try to live and love apart from God that we wither and die. To love without self-protection we must live connected to Jesus.

Only a Power beyond ourselves enables us to love others well, even when they are wrong or are wronging us. Without the empowering grace of God's Spirit in us it can't be done. But through His grace, it can and must be done.

GRACE FOR AUTONOMY

A third and crucial kind of grace necessary and available to us as recovering codependents is God's *embracing grace* for dealing with our autonomous independence from Him and others. This is perhaps the most unexpected grace of all, because our fist in God's face leaves us altogether deserving of His righteous judgment. The serendipity of His embrace when His Spirit confronts us and we repent of our entrenched autonomy is best illustrated in Jesus' parable of the prodigal son, found in Luke 15:11-32.

Kenneth E. Bailey, who lived in the Middle East and researched peasant life there, illuminates the cultural setting of this parable. According to Bailey, the prodigal's request for his share of his father's inheritance, coming when his father was still in good health, shows the prodigal "as wishing for his father's death. . . . The request is seen as a profound break of relationship between the father and his son."[6] Moreover, the older son's silent agreement to share the inheritance implies that he, too, had broken relationship with his father. The father was bereft of both sons.

After the prodigal descended from prosperity into poverty, he "came to his senses" (verse 17) and decided to return home. Bailey suggested, however, that the prodigal only "repented" of squandering his father's money. "He thinks that if he had not lost the money, he would not have sinned."[7] So the boy's plan is to buy his way back into his father's favor by becoming a hired servant. "As a 'hired servant' he will be a free man with his own income living independently in the local village. . . . He can maintain his pride and his independence. . . . In short, he will save himself. He wants no grace."[8]

Like the prodigal, codependents who cling to self-sufficiency and autonomy want no grace, preferring instead to work their own strategies for structuring (or restructuring) their lives. Like the prodigal we are all blithely unaware of the grieving heart of God, a heart broken not just by our destructive lifestyles, but by our refusal to cast ourselves on His mercy and rekindle relationship with Him. *We have "repented" our mistakes and their consequences, but not our wounding of God and others*. We've not listened to the heartbeat of the Father who keeps anguished vigil at the door of Heaven for our return. He yearns to show us grace, but we come with intentions of repayment.

When the prodigal's father humiliated himself by running to meet his son (Oriental noblemen *never* run), embracing him instead of disowning him, he revealed a grace that longs more for relationship than restitution. The prodigal was drawn to genuine repentance and grace, not when he recognized his foolishness, but when he received his father's welcome and abandoned his self-sufficient offer to become a hired servant (compare verses 19 and 21). What the father wanted (and what our heavenly Father wants) is not a servant but a son, and the evidence of the prodigal's true repentance was his joy at receiving restoration of relationship with his father.

Unfortunately, the older brother was more resistant to grace. His public insult of his father (by refusing to come in to his brother's party) put him as much in need of repentance and grace as the prodigal had been. When the father humiliated himself a second time by coming out to plead for his older son's reconciliation toward himself and toward the prodigal, he was met with anger and a bitter complaint that his "servanthood" over the years had gained him nothing of what he really wanted—to party with his friends. This son understood no more of his father's heart than did the prodigal. What is worse, the older son seems not to have cared about his father's heart.

Codependents generally identify more with the older son than with the prodigal. They believe God is more concerned about external obedience than about a person's relationship with Him and with others. The slave mentality (as in the older son) is as grievous to God as open rebellion (as in the prodigal). Bailey said of the two sons: "Both rebel. Both break the father's heart. Both end up in a far country, one physically, the other spiritually. The same unexpected love is demonstrated in humiliation to each. For both this love is crucial if servants are to become sons."[9]

Said another way, God's embracing grace is crucial if codependents are to become trusting children of the Father.

RECEIVED, NOT ACHIEVED

Perhaps the most wonderful and yet most difficult-to-accept aspect of grace is that it cannot be achieved. By its very definition it is beyond our control, and our natural tendency as codependents is to embrace only what we *can* control. It is both comfort and humiliation to realize that nothing in us can merit God's blessings. The Apostle John declared, "Yet to all who *received* [Jesus], to those who believed in his name, he gave the right to become children of God" (John 1:12, emphasis added). Much as we dislike admitting it, we have no right to demand anything of God, nor can we manage without Him. We desperately need His grace—grace that terrifies because it strips us of every semblance of control over our world. "Grace threatens all my normalities,"[10] writes Gerald May, and he is right. I normally try to manage other people and my own inner longings through my codependent strategies—strategies I'm comfortable with and trust a lot. It's "abnormal" for me to depend on God, to trust not in my own competence but in God's grace. Grace, though freely given, is not easily received by those accustomed to achieving.

SUMMING UP

When recovering codependents recognize the need for grieving their losses, pretense, and autonomous independence, they also come to recognize the absolute necessity of receiving God's grace—of help beyond themselves that will offer them a solution. The diagram for recovery now looks like this:

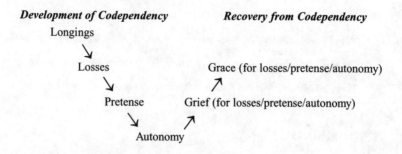

Development of Codependency   **Recovery from Codependency**

Longings

Losses   Grace (for losses/pretense/autonomy)

Pretense   Grief (for losses/pretense/autonomy)

Autonomy

Grace demands nothing of us in payment, but everything of us in trust. My entire way of life is threatened when I depend on God's grace alone. The next chapter will examine the benefits and responsibilities of radical dependence on God.

QUESTIONS FOR BUILDING COMMUNITY

1. Why is it essential for codependents to take Step One of AA's Twelve-Step Program?
2. Explain: Step Two acknowledges the codependent's desperate need for grace.
3. Why is God's *forgiving grace* through Christ's death on the cross foundational to all other graces we experience from Him?
4. Briefly describe an experience you have had (or wish you had had) of God's *comforting grace.*
5. Briefly describe an experience you have had (or wish you had had) of God's *empowering grace.*
6. What was the difference between the prodigal's repentance in the pigpen and his repentance in his father's embrace? How does this apply particularly to codependents?
7. Briefly describe an experience you have had (or wish you had had) of God's *embracing grace.*
8. What codependent characteristics in your own life most frequently block the flow of God's grace *toward* you? The flow of God's grace *through* you?

NOTES

1. Gerald G. May, *Addiction and Grace* (San Francisco, CA: Harper & Row, Publishers, 1988), page 11.
2. May, page 16.

3. Melody Beattie, *Codependent No More* (New York: Harper & Row, Publishers, 1987), page 171.
4. Steve Brown, pastor of Key Biscayne Presbyterian Church in Key Biscayne, Florida, in a sermon on February 18, 1990.
5. David A. Seamands, *Healing Grace* (Wheaton, IL: Scripture Press Publications, 1988), page 109.
6. Kenneth E. Bailey, *Poet and Peasant* and *Through Peasant Eyes* (Grand Rapids, MI: William B. Eerdmans Publishing Company, 1983), page 161.
7. Bailey, page 176.
8. Bailey, page 177.
9. Bailey, page 203.
10. May, page 127.

13

THE FREEDOM OF SURRENDER

❦

Our deserts teach us about the limits of our personal power
and point us toward that constant center of ourselves where
our dignity is found in our dependence upon God.
GERALD G. MAY
Addiction and Grace

When I was eleven or twelve years old, my sister and I spent a summer afternoon at a lake near our house with our cousin, Linda. Linda was the impulsive madcap of the clan, and that day she dared us to race her to the floating dock several hundred feet offshore. Being a novice swimmer, I considered briefly the folly of this adventure, but my companions were smirking and my competence was at stake, so I struck out for the dock in their wake. Exhausted but relieved when I finally grasped the bobbing barrels supporting the dock, I knew with cold certainty it was unlikely I'd make it back to standing-up territory. Nonetheless, ashamed to admit my terror, I frantically followed the others back toward shore.

I don't know how far I got before I ran out of strength and began to flounder in the water. I don't recall shouting for help. I do remember the panic in my soul and the horror on Linda's face as she tried to save me and was dragged down by my clutching. And for some odd reason I have a clear memory of her white bathing cap in my clenched fist as I submerged for what felt like the last time.

Then suddenly strong arms out of nowhere lifted me out of the water so I could gasp and not breathe liquid. I don't know who he was nor what he said—he did speak to me, comforting or chiding, I don't remember which. I can't recall his carrying me to shallow water; I was too busy gulping air and reassuring my brain I wasn't dying. By the time my panic subsided, my rescuer was gone and I was left in knee-deep water feeling foolish.

Yes, *foolish*. I suppose I should have felt grateful, and I *was* glad to be alive. But the prevailing emotion was shame. I had tried to do what I couldn't accomplish, and I was profoundly embarrassed. My cousin didn't have to make fun of me for failing her dare; I was utterly abashed without her words. Instead of thanking the man who'd saved me, I hung my head for not having saved myself.

That incident and its attending emotions picture the codependent's congenital self-sufficiency toward God's offer of redeeming grace. We're drowning and need a savior, but we're embarrassed at our inability to save ourselves. Of course our embarrassment is irrelevant—we need help, like it or not. But our shame often keeps us from asking for and receiving that help—or being grateful for it.

Genuine recovery from codependency is found not in freeing ourselves from needing but in receiving grace. The cost of our freedom is radical dependence on God, which flies in the face of our self-reliance and autonomy. David Seamands contended, "It's hard for Americans to think any good could come out of a dependent relationship, but that's what grace is all about."[1] In order to be free, we have to depend utterly on the God of grace.

In fact, God at times allows us to get in over our heads just to show us our need for Him. Steve Brown once said, "Whatever forces us to our knees, clinging to God, is an asset, not a liability."[2] Unless we are driven to dependence, we will not experience grace.

STEP THREE

Recovering codependents must be willing to renounce on a daily basis their congenital self-reliance. That's what the first two steps in the AA recovery program are all about. The third step speaks of surrender to and dependence on God when it affirms that we *"made a decision to turn our will and our lives over to the care of God as we understood him."* Codependents typically insist that they remain strictly in control of their lives, and it requires a major shift in life strategy for them to relinquish that control to the care of God.

However, if we're to put God in charge of our will and life, we ought to be asking what kind of God He is. Can He be trusted to really *care* for us, as this step suggests?

GOD MISUNDERSTOOD

Ever since the Garden of Eden the Serpent has been bent on maligning God's character—sometimes blatantly, sometimes subtly. A favorite strategy for distorting the truth about God is through unhealthy parental modeling. We receive our earliest and most profoundly believed ideas about God through watching our parents, particularly our fathers. A child who grows up with a distant, unresponsive father believes God is like that, too. A child who cannot please his or her parents will see God as unpleasable as well. Worst of all, when parents abuse or neglect their children, those children's concept of God will be profoundly twisted, and they will emotionally (if not intellectually) view God as harsh, vindictive, or perhaps even evil.

The child's wrong concepts of God formed by disappointing experiences with his or her parents, may keep the child from even wanting a relationship with God as an adult. If we are to take Step Three and turn our will and lives over to God's care, we must discover what God is really like.

REVEALED TRUTH ABOUT GOD

A friend of mine once said, "God is not made of Play-Doh. We can't just fashion Him into whatever shape suits our fancy." How true. God is who He is, not who we want Him to be. And He reveals who He is and what He's like in the Bible. It is in Scripture we learn of His attributes—His justice, mercy, wisdom, sovereignty, holiness, goodness, love, and so on. Of course, reading about God won't change our emotions toward Him. Yet it is essential to know where the truth about God (what Scripture reveals to our mind) contradicts what we feel about God (based on our childhood misconceptions) so we can make responsible choices about what to believe and how to act in relationship to Him.

Nowhere is God's nature seen more clearly than in the life of Jesus, God's Son made flesh to dwell among us. A. W. Tozer reminded us that "Christ walked with men on earth that He might show them what God is like and make known the true nature of God to a race that had wrong ideas about Him. This was only one of the things He did while here in the flesh, but this He did with beautiful perfection."[3] By observing Jesus' words and actions in the gospels we glimpse the wonderful goodness, justice, and grace of our Father-God. Jesus Himself declared, "Anyone who has seen me has seen the Father" (John 14:9). If we want our misconceptions about God cleared up, we would do well to look at Jesus.

GOD AS FATHER

Because our codependency often flows out of the losses we experienced in abusive or neglectful families, we tend to hold skewed notions of God as Father. An important part of my own recovery process is experiencing a redeemed Parent-child relationship with God, seeing myself as His beloved daughter and practicing a childlike relationship with Him in my spiritual walk. Young children have nothing to offer but themselves—their need, their trust, and their love. In His grace God reduces me to the raw nakedness of needing and receiving—the stuff of children, even infants. And I'm finding His Father-care wonderful beyond the telling of it.

Step Three calls us to turn our lives over to God's care, and good fathers do care for their children. Therefore, as recovering codependents we can profit from exploring the traits of God that reveal Him as a most wonderful Father.[4]

First, though it seems obvious, God reveals Himself in Scripture as a *Person*, not an inanimate force or idea. The personal nature of the God of the Bible calls out to our own nature as persons who long for relationship. Good fathers interact with their children in ways that affirm their children's value as human beings, just as God in Scripture interacted with His children, beginning with Adam and Eve and continuing with countless men and women throughout the Old and New Testaments. Moses reminded the Israelites of this just before they entered Canaan: "You saw how the LORD your God carried you, as a father carries his son, all the way you went until you reached this place" (Deuteronomy 1:31).

A second attribute of our Father-God is His *justice*. Parents who fail to set or enforce high standards do their children great damage. Children want their parents to do right, and they're disappointed and embarrassed when their parents are morally lax—toward themselves or toward their children. Kids thrive on discipline, not permissiveness. The writer of Proverbs says,

> My son, do not despise the LORD's discipline
>   and do not resent his rebuke,
> because the LORD disciplines those he loves,
>   as a father the son he delights in.
>   (Proverbs 3:11-12)

Bill and I show our love for Christopher well when we stand in the way of his foolishness. More and more I feel loved by God when He stands in the way of *my* foolishness. What flows from His Spirit as He rebukes my sin is not hatred but concern, not vengeance but compassion. He loves me too much to let my continued rebellion (which would ultimately destroy me) go unchallenged.

For those who were never disciplined as children or who were abused in the name of "discipline," it's important to see God's justice in the context of His love: He cares enough about our good character to lovingly correct us when we're wrong. It won't hurt any less, but we can trust the love that motivates it.

That brings us to the third character quality of our Father-God: His *unfailing love*. The psalmist exulted: "The LORD is good and his love endures forever" (Psalm 100:5). A good father offers love to his child through his acceptance of and delight in his child. God is pleased to have a relationship with me as His child, perhaps in the same way Bill and I often delight in our relationship with Christopher. The prophet Zephaniah promised that the Father "will take great delight in you, he will quiet you with his love, he will rejoice over you with singing" (Zephaniah 3:17). A good father also offers love through his affection, both verbal and physical, and gladly forgives his child when he or she repents. As the prodigal son was embraced by his father, so our heavenly Father longs to embrace us every time we return to Him. Countless times I have looked into His face and have seen the delight of His greeting. The Aaronic blessing is one of my favorites:

> The LORD bless you
>   and keep you;

the LORD make his face shine upon you
    and be gracious to you;
the LORD turn his face toward you
    and give you peace.
        (Numbers 6:24-26)

I have come to treasure the thought of my heavenly Father's face turned toward me.

One of the most profound effects of being deeply connected to God is a renewed sense of our own preciousness. When I know and can believe God cherishes me as a beloved child, I can know and believe in my worth as a person. A young child learns to place value on whatever his or her parents value; that is why parental neglect or abuse is so devastating to the self-esteem of a child. Self-worth is a byproduct of consistent love from one's parents or other significant adult; children can't generate it themselves.

But as we experience God's steady love for us as His precious children, we begin to place that same value on ourselves. Self-love only flows from being loved. Scripture doesn't command self-love but assumes it as the natural byproduct of our being the recipients of God's love. We are children of the Great King and special to our Father. Princes and princesses don't let themselves be abused; they like themselves and expect to be respected. D. Martyn Lloyd-Jones reminds us: "The most wonderful thing of all is not that my sins have been forgiven, nor that I may enjoy certain experiences and blessings as a Christian. The thing that should astound me . . . is that I am a child of God, one of God's people."[5] Our status as children of God, connected to Him by bonds of Father-love, has many benefits, one of which is the self-valuing that flows from contact with a perfect heavenly Father. He loves us a whole lot for His own Name's sake.

Finally, God is a God of *sovereign strength.* Our connectedness with Him is not a connection of equals. God being God and we being created by Him makes us contingent creatures, dependent on Him. He has the right to rule simply because He is God, but He always uses His strength to accomplish good for His children. The psalmist declared, "God is our refuge and strength, an ever-present help in trouble" (Psalm 46:1). A good father is like that, too, strong enough not to be bullied by his children nor to lean on them, but also using His strength in their behalf—to offer them the provision and protection they need.

Those codependents whose fathers disappointed them may find it difficult to turn their will and lives over to God's care. But as we correct our misconceptions about Him through a study of Scripture and time spent quietly in His presence, we'll grow to trust Him more and to find an increasing freedom to be authentic—to experience, perhaps for the first time, what it's like to rest in the arms of a good Father who cares deeply for us and is committed to our good.

SURRENDER

Because we were made for relationship with God, we as recovering codependents "come home" to our true self when we surrender our will and turn our life over to the care of our heavenly Father. Just as children in healthy homes lean wholeheartedly and unself-consciously on their parents, so we, too, must more and more depend on God for all that we need.

Jesus is our model for God-dependent living. His every word and action had its foundation in His reliance on the Father. "For I did not speak of my own accord, but the Father who sent me commanded me what to say and how to say it. . . . Whatever I say is just what the Father has told me to say," Jesus said to His followers (John 12:49-50). His intimate fellowship with God was the wellspring out of which flowed the grace He offered to those He encountered. Listen to Jesus' own words about His dependence on His Father: "I tell you the truth, the Son can do nothing by himself; he can do only what he sees his Father doing, because whatever the Father does the Son also does" (John 5:19). The Son of God, who had life in Himself (John 1:4), was nevertheless utterly dependent on the Father's life in Him to know what to say and how to act. We're called to depend on God in the same way.

Surrender to God may mean different things to different codependents. This is what I understand by the term:

Surrender means a person enters life through faith in Christ's atoning death and sustains life by daily abiding in grace (i.e., God's acceptance, forgiveness, and empowerment through the Holy Spirit), resulting in spiritual vitality, a sense of place and worth, and the potential for intimacy.

Let's examine this definition of surrender.

ENTERING AND SUSTAINING LIFE

When a person receives God's gift of atonement through faith in Christ's death on his behalf, that person moves from darkness to light, from death into life. Moses urged the Israelites to "choose life, so that you and your children may live and that you may love the LORD your God, listen to his voice, and hold fast to him. For the LORD is your life" (Deuteronomy 30:19-20). Connection with God has always meant life, and separation from Him has always meant death. When we enter renewed fellowship with God through faith in Christ, we have within us the Life Jesus had in Him, the Life of God.

We sustain that life by relying on and abiding daily in grace (God's acceptance, forgiveness, and empowerment through the Holy Spirit). When we make what David Needham calls a Declaration of Dependence, we receive through the Spirit the grace of God's very Life: "Of course such a life will express itself in righteous acts, but the foundation for those acts is *dependence*. Not in the sense of God helping us, but in God living through us."[6] It is God's life expressed through our individual, unique, redeemed personalities and giftedness that constitutes our surrender to God and our utter dependence on Him. Bible-reading, prayer, fellowship, and the sacraments all minister grace to us, but it is God operating in our spirit through those things that makes us truly alive.

BENEFITS OF SURRENDER

The most crucial benefit of surrendering our will and our life to God is spiritual vitality—the reality of a new inner life in our spirit. The Apostle John insisted that only those connected to Jesus by faith have genuine life: "He who has the Son has life; he who does not have the Son of God does not have life" (1 John 5:12). Codependency is a *way of life*, but God-dependence offers us Life itself, allowing us to reclaim our true humanity.

A second major benefit of surrender is belonging in God's family without having to "earn our keep." We are children of God through our faith in Christ (John 1:12), and our inheritance is the sense of belonging, worth, and serenity associated with our new status. We have an uncontested place in a loving and committed family, the Church of Christ. We can know ourselves to be persons of worth because we've been bought with Jesus' blood, our value rooted in the efficacy of His death on our behalf.

The serenity of Jesus' life even in the midst of tension is mute evidence of His dependence on the Father. We codependents are relentlessly frantic in reacting to people and circumstances, trying desperately to manage our world. On a recent business trip I took a shuttle van from downtown Chicago to O'Hare International Airport, and the ride was without doubt one of the worst I had ever experienced. The driver drove as though he had a nervous tic in his right foot, accelerating then decelerating on the average of ten times per minute (I counted them while watching his digital clock), regardless of the flow of traffic around him. Back and forth my head jerked; his record was sixteen accelerations in one minute—that's thirty-two head jerks. My neck was sore for two days.

Codependents live like that a lot, always reacting to others' expectations and trying to compensate for the pull in a dozen directions. They ache all the time from their efforts at world-management. Jesus' gracious word to them is this: "Come to me, all you who are weary and burdened, and I will give you rest" (Matthew 11:28). We don't have to hold everything together anymore. We can rest in Jesus' care and turn our burdens over to Him, knowing He will work all things for our good as we become more like Him (Romans 8:28-29). Serenity is available to God's children who depend utterly on Him.

A third benefit of surrender is the freedom to embrace genuine intimacy. Our deepest fear of abandonment (by God) will, because of Calvary, never happen, so we can risk being who we really are with other people. Even if we're rejected by others, we can rest in knowing we're accepted by the Father. Rejection will hurt, but we really will survive if we lean on Him. Depending utterly on God for our ultimate well-being is the doorway to intimacy, to a renewed freedom to love, to hurt, to laugh, to make mistakes, to ask forgiveness, to feel our feelings, to start each day new. We're free in Him to finally be alive.

But with freedom comes responsibility. God hasn't freed us to become self-centered. He calls us out of codependent bondage so we can bond with others in mutual interdependence. He offers us grace so we can risk offering it to others.

SUMMING UP

We have almost completed our diagram outlining the development of and recovery from codependency. It looks like this:

Development of Codependency	*Recovery from Codependency*
Longings	Surrender (of life and will)
Losses	Grace (for losses/pretense/autonomy)
Pretense	Grief (for losses/pretense/autonomy)
Autonomy	

Surrendering our will and life to God, though utterly reliable because of His immutable character, is a dangerous way to live. It's not just that we fear God might not "be there" for us when life disappoints or damages us—and He typically isn't "there" in the way or to the degree we want and expect. The danger is deeper, touching us at our most frightening levels of helplessness.

If I depend on God alone, I must turn and face everything I've run from as a codependent all my life. I must enter the abject humiliation of needing, of asking for what my soul longs for, instead of protecting myself from the pain of its loss. I must embrace the terror of aloneness, the possibility that no one will understand or approve of me except God. I must live without control over the people and circumstances of my life, freeing others to choose to respond to me positively or negatively—or not at all—without medicating my pain.

Most of all, surrendering to God requires that I fully own my personal responsibility to love others well. He asks me to abandon my cherished notions of contempt for myself and others and to risk moving with His strength into others' lives, intent on doing them good. The next chapter will examine in greater detail how depending on God involves the risk-taking of mutual interdependence.

QUESTIONS FOR BUILDING COMMUNITY

1. How does the near-drowning episode described at the beginning of this chapter illustrate the codependent's typical attitude toward depending on God?
2. Why do codependents (even recovering codependents) resist taking AA's Step Three?
3. Which attribute of God was best modeled by your parent(s)? Which was least modeled by your parent(s)?
4. Tell why it is easy or difficult for you to think of God as your Father.
5. Describe something you wish your father or mother would do (or had done) for you. Can you imagine God filling in that gap for you as your Father?
6. Give some examples of ways in which we act as though God were made of Play-Doh.
7. Think of a way God has confronted you recently with your sin. Did that confirm or contradict His love for you? Explain.
8. Think of your own codependent strategies and tell what it might look like if you were to abandon them and enjoy instead the peace of surrendering your will and life to the care of God.

NOTES
1. David A. Seamands, *Healing Grace* (Wheaton, IL: Scripture Press Publications, 1988), page 32.
2. Steve Brown, pastor of Key Biscayne Presbyterian Church in Key Biscayne, Florida, in a sermon on June 23, 1988.
3. A. W. Tozer, *The Knowledge of the Holy* (San Francisco, CA: Harper & Row, Publishers, 1961), page 90.
4. For a thorough discussion of God's attributes as a Father and how our concept of Him can be distorted by childhood experiences, see the excellent book by Phil Davis, *The Father I Never Knew: Finding the Perfect Parent in God* (Colorado Springs, CO: NavPress, 1991).
5. D. Martyn Lloyd-Jones, as quoted in *Christianity Today*, April 23, 1990, page 33.
6. David C. Needham, *Birthright: Christian, Do You Know Who You Are?* (Portland, OR: Multnomah Press, 1979), page 104.

PART FOUR

WHAT DOES BONDING LOOK LIKE?

14

RECIPROCAL GRACE:
FREE TO LOVE AND FORGIVE

❦

*There are some needs that can only be met through
interaction with another person, . . . [and] it is our
responsibility to recognize those needs and ask someone
appropriate to meet them. We in turn must learn to meet
others' needs at appropriate times in proper
circumstances, which is called interdependence.*
PIA MELLODY, ANDREA WELLS MILLER,
J. KEITH MILLER
Facing Codependence

When God brings us out of our codependency through the process of grief and grace into dependence on Him, He also calls us to mutual interdependence. But, escaping codependency and embracing biblical love won't be easy. We'll suffer the exquisite pain of withdrawal from our relationship addictions, our codependency screaming at us to resume our former way of life. We'll even grieve the death of our codependency as a familiar and comfortable friend. Living in appropriate dependence on God and others requires painful choices as we wrestle old habits into conformity with our new identity in Christ.

The first three steps of AA's Twelve-Step program trace the necessity of personal brokenness and reliance on God as prerequisites for recovery from codependency. The remaining nine AA steps describe what we must do to maintain our recovery.

However, a word of caution: Replacing our former bondage to addiction or codependency with a new set of rules (which AA's Twelve Steps could become) will not lead us into life. The saving grace made available to us through Jesus' atoning death isn't named in most Twelve-Step programs, but it is essential if we're to enjoy God's restoration from our codependent bondage. Sobriety and interdependence, while preferable to drunkenness and codependency, are not synonymous with biblical redemption. The Twelve Steps describe many of the changes grace brings to our lives, but they cannot substitute for grace nor make grace happen. Grace is never negotiable. We cannot command grace but only receive it. We cannot program life but only live it. We cannot force relationships but only open ourselves to them.

The grace offered us through our new life in Christ bonds us to God and becomes ours to offer others; if they choose, they can bond with us, too. But we cannot force our way. Newborn babies instinctively bond with their primary caregivers, but adults make choices about whom they love. The rest of this book explores our movement from bondage to bonding, but with the realization that bonding is a mysterious union requiring (in adults) two consenting partners.

The reciprocity of our loving involvement with God and those around us is based on a crucial assumption—i.e., *that each partner in the relationship is a separate person taking the full responsibility of individual selfhood.* Sometimes that establishment of selfhood must begin with detachment.

DETACHMENT

Detachment refers to a codependent's temporary emotional distancing from an enmeshed relationship for the purpose of examining what is making the relationship unhealthy. It may look like autonomous independence and may in fact *become* that unless its goal is ultimately to reattach in an appropriate way and to learn to love correctly. To detach, codependents must invite others to help them gain perspective on and grieve over how they have failed to genuinely love.

Love cannot flourish in the presence of unchallenged abuse or addiction. Parents with a drug-addicted daughter show her no love by giving her a monthly allowance. A man fails to love his alcoholic wife by viewing her drinking as his personal cross to bear and refusing to confront the destructiveness of her alcoholism. A wife whose work-addicted husband neglects the family isn't loving him when she silently takes up the slack for him. People who enable their loved ones to remain in their addictions are in bondage to their own codependent behavior, and their choices fall radically short of Jesus' strong, confrontive love.

A time of detachment allows codependents to step back emotionally and face the destructiveness of their own style of relating. They are accustomed to focusing on how *they* have been damaged. But they must also repent of the damage they have done by their codependent enabling, which flows from their fear of confrontation or loss, not from their commitment to the other's ultimate good.

Detachment involves a codependent's decision to confront the addict's behavior and to refuse the abuse that has accompanied it. In some cases it may include physically leaving a relationship for a season to break the abusive cycle. However, abandoning the relationship, although the relief from the constant pain the relationship has caused may be tempting, may not be the right (i.e., the loving) thing to do. Many enablers run from their enmeshed relationships to free themselves from dysfunction, refusing to face their own love failures and ignoring the deeper issues of their autonomy and God's claim on their loving obedience. Moreover, they often discover later that the problem wasn't the addict, but their own wrong way of relating to the addict. The codependent's relational pattern won't be changed by leaving; it will simply reappear in future relationships if it isn't dealt with.

Removing oneself from a painful relationship may bring relief, but the relief may remove the codependent from a desperate dependence on God. Our determination to stop the pain and manage our lives without God sabotages our ultimate good, which is the daily surrender of our life and will to His care. Our redeemed nature also draws us to love others as we love ourselves, and we reach toward that new nature when we commit ourselves to move beyond detachment to mutual interdependence.

COSTLY COMMITMENT

I remember the pain of my own commitment to reattach after I had detached from Bill. Things were so bad I thought I couldn't go on, and I was ready for divorce. A good friend, however, counseled me otherwise.

"I know how much pain you're in," she said, "but if you run from this relationship now, you won't learn your most important lesson—how to love Bill right. If you face your pain and keep confronting Bill in love, God will honor your faithfulness and heal you within the context of your suffering—and maybe change Bill's heart."

She was right. Staying with Bill during that time was one of the hardest things I've ever done. But I needed to learn a deeper dependence on God, and He showed Himself strong on my behalf in those dark days. And when Bill eventually began his own spiritual journey toward healing, I was deeply grateful to be able to share it with him. Not all codependents who confront in love are blessed with healing in their most intimate relationships, but all can find God's presence in the pain and the guidance of God's Spirit in choosing the right path.

DEFINITION OF MUTUAL INTERDEPENDENCE

God created us for and calls us to dependence on Him and mutual interdependence with one another. But just what is mutual interdependence? Consider this definition:

Mutual interdependence occurs when two persons, secure in God's acceptance, mutually give and receive love and forgiveness without demanding approval or conformity to expectations in return, resulting in spiritual vitality, a balanced view of self, and genuine intimacy.

The definition bears closer examination.

ROOTED IN GOD'S LOVE

Mutual interdependence happens best in the context of two persons who have experienced God's acceptance through Christ. The grace flowing from God into their individual lives overflows into each other's lives. Secure in their status before God, they no longer need to demand that the other change or offer them the approval for which they long. They can love not from deficit but from an abundance of grace.

Recovering codependents must test out this reality time and again. In the vacuum left by their abandoned strategies of self-protection and control, they must risk believing God's acceptance is adequate in the absence of others' approval, His love enough when others reject them. Their aloneness with God will both exhilarate and terrify. Though their utter dependence on Him is crucial to their mutual interdependence, their neediness will feel like death. The challenge will be to act on the reality that it is, in fact, life.

MUTUALITY

The goal of every relationship should be mutuality of growth and grace. During the early stages of recovery from codependency this is almost never the case; usually one person changes and grows before the other is willing or able to follow suit. The person who begins the process must not fall into a self-righteous pattern of always giving and never receiving but must remain committed to the goal of reciprocal grace flowing back and forth in the relationship.

Crucial to this balanced view of mutual interdependence is the codependent's ability to determine the legitimate responsibilities of each person in the relationship. Codependents have been accustomed to either giving too much or too little in a relationship and often don't know what is appropriate to offer or receive. Feedback from a support group helps recovering codependents learn give-and-take in their relationships, based on what is good for both themselves and the person they are learning to love in a more biblical way.

MUTUAL LOVE

Love is the first reciprocally enjoyed gift of mutual interdependence. The word connotes romantic feelings or warm fuzzies toward the codependent's "significant other," but if limited to such a definition, many codependents rightly conclude that their relationships are doomed because none of those feelings are left after years of abuse and disappointment. *If, however, love is not ultimately an emotion but a commitment to aggressively pursuing the other person's welfare, then love is a choice we can make even toward someone we don't feel particularly close to.* Acting in someone else's best interest approaches what Jesus did (not felt) in laying down His life for His beloved. It is the love God requires when He commands us to love our neighbor as ourselves—not to create more loving feelings, but to determine what is in our neighbor's best interest and then do it.

Recovering codependents express their love in two ways. The Apostle Paul refers to them as "[taking] off your old self with its practices" and "[putting] on the new self, which is being renewed in knowledge in the image of its Creator" (Colossians 3:9-10). As children of the Great King we are to take off the beggar's rags we've been wearing and clothe ourselves with garments befitting our royal heritage.

Putting off Codependency

Putting off the beggar's rags means we renounce and discontinue the codependent behaviors on which we've built our lives. We can stop our self-deception by facing what is in our souls and being who we really are without pretense about our pain or sin. We can abandon our self-sufficiency and admit we need God and others in order to live fully. Our self-aggrandizement can give way to letting others make their own choices and live with the consequences of those choices. We can renounce our self-contempt and our self-forfeiture, offering the substance of our souls to bless the ones we're committed to loving. If we are connected to God and leaning desperately on Him, we can stop doing codependent things—it's as simple as taking off ragged clothes.

Putting on Biblical Love

On the positive side, putting on royal garments refers to Christlike behaviors we practice even when we don't particularly feel like it. This doesn't mean we ignore our negative feelings, but that we acknowledge them to God with integrity and intensity, and then choose to behave as He directs us through His Word and Spirit. That's what Jesus did in the Garden of Gethsemane.

Here's what Paul told the believers in Colosse: "Therefore, as God's chosen people, holy and dearly loved, clothe yourselves with compassion, kindness, humility, gentleness and patience" (Colossians 3:12). As redeemed codependents we can put on compassion toward other people's pain because we've learned (finally) to linger in our own. We can practice kindness because we no longer have to punish or control those who have disappointed us. We recognize that humility consists not in denying our power but in acknowledging that it comes from God. Gentleness is possible even when rebuking those who harm us, because we know our purpose is not to destroy but to redeem. And patience becomes our habit because we know God isn't finished with any of us yet, and because His presence enables us to endure our fiery trials with perseverance, if not always tranquility. We don't "dress up" in Christlike behaviors to pretend we're royalty, but to show we already are. Because Christ dwells within us, we can choose to act like Him.

RECIPROCAL FORGIVENESS

A second precious gift we offer each other when we become mutually interdependent is forgiveness. Forgiveness is the heartbeat of any love relationship. It has three essential ingredients.

Loving Confrontation

The first ingredient of forgiveness is loving confrontation. Codependents think it unloving (and certainly dangerous) to risk genuine honesty about how others have damaged or abused them. It's safer to take the blame, swallow the hurt, and just "forgive and forget." But it's more loving—and more respectful—to hold others accountable. When codependents set appropriate boundaries for themselves by refusing to accept mistreatment, they are doing what is good not just for themselves but for their abusers as well. A recovering codependent who says without apology, "You may not mistreat me anymore!" is loving others well because abuse damages both victim and agent. But setting limits and reestablishing boundaries meet the criteria for biblical love only if the focus is on mutual welfare, not revenge or personal safety.

Forgiveness and restoration are impossible if sin is not addressed. Jesus didn't forgive without confrontation. His uncompromising message, like John the Baptist's, was one of repentance (Matthew 4:17). Jesus spoke and did what was for others' good at His own expense; we must do the same.

And we *will* pay when we confront the abuse we've been indulging. Codependents who want to love right must risk others' anger and disapproval by describing how they have been sinned against, and it will upset the status quo. They must also, however, be willing to hear how they have sinned against others, how their attitudes and behaviors have damaged people's lives. There must be mutuality of honesty about the impact of sin in the relationship.

Repentance

The second ingredient of forgiveness is repentance. Jesus made it clear: "If your brother sins, rebuke him, and *if he repents*, forgive him" (Luke

17:3, emphasis added). Without repentance, there is no forgiveness. God requires it; so should we. Repentance is not apology (though it may involve apology), but a turning of the heart back toward God and toward a commitment to the other's welfare. A superficial "I'm sorry" deserves no forgiveness; it doesn't satisy God, either. "Produce fruit in keeping with repentance," warned John the Baptist (Matthew 3:8). Words are cheap, and we would much prefer to offer a shallow apology than to come face to face with our heinous sins of betrayal and rebellion. Yet our memories of grace both entice and empower us to open ourselves to the Spirit's convicting so we can turn our hearts back toward God and others time and time again.

However, repentance is not penance, either. There is a distinction between living out one's repentance in genuine behavior changes and groveling for restoration by promising to "make it all up to you." Recovering codependents should expect the former without demanding the latter.

Sometimes one partner must wait a long time for the other's repentance. I was ready to forgive Bill before he was ready to request or receive my forgiveness. As long as he couldn't admit his damage of me, he couldn't repent and I couldn't restore him to right relationship with me. I have a dear friend who in a similar way waited for me to acknowledge how I had wounded her, enduring on my behalf the pain of a waiting love. My repentance toward her, when it came, opened the door to sweet renewal of friendship between us, as did Bill's eventual repentance toward me.

Grace

In the presence of honest confrontation and genuine repentance, grace is the crowning glory of forgiveness. God models it: When the Holy Spirit convicts us and we turn from our sin, the Father offers us His grace in Christ, welcoming us back into fellowship with Himself. Grace cancels the debt owed and accepts the debtor without seeking revenge. We, too, can offer grace. Because of the damage done to us, mercy from us is undeserved. Yet because we are recipients of God's grace, we offer it to others. *Restoration to relationship, supported by continuing repentance and genuine change, is the ultimate goal of grace.*

Forgiveness is both the hallmark and foundation of genuine intimacy and mutual interdependence. Asking for it requires an absence of pretense or defensiveness, and offering it demands an absence of revenge or emotional blackmail (making the other person pay later on). Forgiveness must be reciprocal, specific, and continual; as long as we live this side of Home, we will always need to seek and offer it to one another.

BENEFITS OF MUTUAL INTERDEPENDENCE

Learning to live in mutual interdependence with others is good for us. One of its greatest benefits is *spiritual vitality*. When learning to love imperfect human beings God's way, we must remain dependent on God and alive to our new spiritual identity in Him (including both our needs and our giftedness). Giving and receiving grace from God and others is the essence of our spirituality. If we are to avoid being Dead Sea persons, we must not just allow grace to flow in (as the Dead Sea receives water from the Jordan River), but we must also allow that grace to flow out into the lives of others (instead of stagnating like the trapped water of the Dead Sea).

A second benefit of mutual interdependence is *a balanced view of self*. Recovering codependents must move from their old self-image (as martyr, rescuer, nobody, victim, etc.) into seeing and living out their new identity in Christ (as lover, encourager, confronter, grace-giver, etc.). We are no one's savior (not even our own), and that's good news because Jesus is all the Savior we need. But we are no one's slave or victim, either; we are new creatures with much to offer others because Jesus' life is a fountain of living water nourishing the lives of us and those around us. We are not just repaired sinners with new power to fight temptation, but adopted children of the heavenly King with an entirely new identity to offer in all of our relationships. We are not worthless; our value has been set by the price paid for us—the blood of the precious Son of God. We are not God, but God's life is flowing through us because of the Holy Spirit's union with our spirit. That balanced view of self as precious but utterly dependent on God is a wonderful benefit codependents receive as they live out their new identity in mutual interdependence.

Finally, mutual interdependence affords us a taste in this life of *genuine intimacy*. Because we were built to love God, others, and ourselves, we are expressing our truest self when we enter and sustain

mutually interdependent relationships with one another. Genuine intimacy involves freedom, authenticity, acceptance, and forgiveness; all
are made possible through surrender and dependence on God, and all
are experienced in freely chosen interdependence with others.

SUMMING UP

Let's take a final look at the chart showing the development of and
recovery from codependency. Note that it is cyclical—i.e., in order to
avoid going down into autonomy and self-preoccupation, recovering
codependents must move again and again into recognizing their longings, losses, and pretense, then move up through the stages of grief,
grace, and surrender into mutual interdependence. The process is not
once-and-for-all, but repetitive and cyclical.

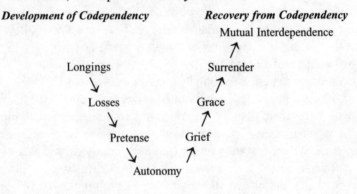

REVIEW OF DEFINITIONS

As we come full circle in our discussion of the recovery process out of
codependency, let's review our major definitions.

Codependency is a self-focused way of life in which a person blind
to his or her true self continually reacts to others, being controlled by
and seeking to control their behavior, attitudes, and/or opinions, resulting in spiritual sterility, loss of authenticity, and absence of intimacy.

Autonomous independence is a self-sufficient way of life in which
a person attempts to self-generate acceptance, forgiveness, and empowerment apart from God, resulting in spiritual rebellion, a distorted view
of self, and problems with intimacy.

Surrender means a person enters life through faith in Christ's atoning death and sustains life by daily abiding in grace (i.e., God's acceptance, forgiveness, and empowerment through the Holy Spirit), resulting in spiritual vitality, a sense of place and worth, and the potential for intimacy.

Mutual interdependence occurs when two persons, secure in God's acceptance, mutually give and receive love and forgiveness without demanding approval or conformity to expectations in return, resulting in spiritual vitality, a balanced view of self, and genuine intimacy.

The rest of this book will consider the practical details of living out appropriate dependence on God and others as an alternative to addiction, codependency, and/or autonomy. Steps Four through Twelve of the AA program will serve as our outline.

QUESTIONS FOR BUILDING COMMUNITY

1. How are dependence on God and mutual interdependence related to Jesus' summary of the Law in Matthew 22:37-40?
2. What is the difference between detachment and autonomous independence?
3. What is the relationship between detachment and mutual interdependence?
4. Why is it important that mutual interdependence be rooted in God's unconditional love?
5. If love is a commitment to aggressively pursuing the other person's good, in what ways is codependency a violation of love? Give some specific examples.
6. Explain: The personal boundaries of a recovering codependent are naturally established by the principles of biblical love.
7. Give specific examples of how a recovering codependent can "put off" the following characteristics:
   a. self-forfeiture,
   b. self-contempt,
   c. self-aggrandizement,
   d. self-sufficiency,
   e. self-deception.
8. How is a recovering codependent's expectation of repentance (before restoration) different from demanding change?

15

COURAGEOUS VULNERABILITY: FREE TO ABANDON DENIAL

❦

*If the Lord Jesus came to give life, and life abundant, then
a life of pretense involves a clear denial of the gospel, no
matter how moral, virtuous, or appealing that life may seem.*
DAN ALLENDER
The Wounded Heart

People who live in South Florida with its hot, muggy weather spend most of their time in air-conditioned cars or in buildings with darkened windows. Emerging into daylight is always a shock, not just because of the heat and humidity, but also because of the blinding brightness. The adjustment can take a while.

So it is when we emerge from denial to live out our lives of grace. It's a shock to see things in the glaring light of reality instead of the dark colors of delusion. The self, hidden behind closed drapes for years, is unaccustomed to the light of vulnerability and won't expect to be loved. In fact, we'll need God's grace just to crack the door to self-discovery and self-disclosure.

But, as David Seamands reminded us, grace "can make you strong enough and brave enough to *take off your superself mask and begin to look at your real self.* For it's your real self which God loves and for which Christ died, your real self with all its sins and flaws which He has always known and never stopped loving."[1] The enabling force behind our new honesty is God's unfailing love; He loved us before we knew how bad we were, and He loves us as much now as He did then.

What do we bring into the light of redeemed living as recovering codependents? The development of codependency proceeded along the lines of our longings, losses, pretense, and autonomy. Let's examine what it will mean to come out of denial in each of those areas.

ACKNOWLEDGING OUR TRUE SELVES

First, we must become open about our longings. That means admitting we *have* longings for intimacy with our parents, our spouse, our children, our friends, and of course, God. Admitting our longings is painful because it makes us face the anger and sadness of having those longings betrayed.

Not only must we *admit* our longings; we must also *embrace* them, though it feels like taking fire to our heart. If we run from our legitimate yearnings for intimacy with God and others, we cut ourselves off from being alive. To be at peace with our longings will take time, but true humanness requires that we own and embrace our deep need for genuine intimacy.

TRUTH ABOUT LOSSES

We must also come out of denial about our losses. Where formerly we had numbed our anger and pain at life's disappointments, now we must come to terms with our losses and all their accompanying emotions. I spent most of my life denying the impact my father's alcoholism and my mother's codependency had on me, from my childhood right up to the present time. I engaged in what Timmen Cermak calls "the psychic numbing that makes your life more distant and less real."[2] I simply kept my emotions at arm's length and pretended I wasn't damaged.

Now that I'm facing the anger and sadness of my losses, I find myself shocked by this new and unfamiliar sunlight in my soul. Sometimes I retreat back into the shadowy safety of pretending it wasn't as bad as it was. But I'm learning I can survive in the daylight, and so can my love for my parents and for others who have harmed me. Grace is freeing me to no longer minimize, justify, or deny my losses, but to face them with integrity and grieve over them. Coming out of denial about past losses has been critical to my healing process.

We're called to live without denial about our present losses as well. It's painful but necessary to be alive to every moment's reality, rejoicing over the gifts of grace offered us, grieving the pain of even the minor losses of each day, and repenting the ever-recurring sin of trying to make our lives work without depending utterly on God. And that brings us to a closer look at coming out of denial about our self-protective ego facades.

REALITY ABOUT PRETENSE

We all would like to deny our pretense—the ways we've hidden our real selves behind protective masks, not just from others, but from ourselves as well. We must deliberately open our hearts to the awful and wonderful truth about ourselves, for we've been deluded about our real weaknesses and about our real strengths. We've tried to control things beyond our power to control, and we've believed ourselves powerless when we should have acted boldly. Our ego facades kept us safe from pain but irresponsible about loving appropriately.

One of the most loving gifts we offer in relationships is authenticity. Not long ago a friend sadly remarked about a mutual acquaintance: "Ralph just isn't himself around me." It was true. Ralph was caught up in pretense, trying to convince everyone he was someone he really wasn't. His relationships didn't flow naturally, and he was really a very lonely man. Giving our hearts—being and offering others our true selves, with all our flaws and strengths—is risky business, to be sure. Authenticity is decidedly not safe. But we will never truly bond with anyone with whom we cannot be honest.

It begins with self-honesty, admitting what is real within so that we can offer aliveness and reality to those around us. We must enter our lives courageously, acknowledging our anger, sadness, joy, tenderness, loneliness—whatever *is*, not what should be or what we wish were true. Niceness is not bad, but if it's merely a safe alternative to honesty, we must seek to know what's blocking us from being real. Openness is the only door to genuine bonding.

Step Four in the Twelve-Step program declares that in recovery we *"made a searching and fearless moral inventory of ourselves."* For too long we shrank from taking inventory of our moral life because we wrongly believed our value lay in our perfectibility rather than in our preciousness. Authenticity frees us from that continual backward glance over the shoulder to wonder how we're doing or what others are thinking, and it also offers others that same freedom. It's time we all admitted we're a mess, that we don't do things right very often—and then usually by accident. In the context of God's unfailing mercy, honesty about our particular failures to love opens us not to judgment but to grace. Our inventory will reveal us as worse than we thought we were. But the realization doesn't destroy us, because instead of rejection we find the unexpected steadiness of the Father's compassion toward His children. The discovery is sweet every time.

There is one aspect of the "moral inventory" we often minimize or neglect: the listing of our giftedness. It is easier to disbelieve we have something to offer than to accept responsibility for loving others with strength and compassion. God has gifted us, and we are obliged to bless others with who we are, to love them without resentment or pretense, though we'll inevitably be hurt in the process. Seeing ourselves in the sunlight of reality will include not just acknowledging our love failures, but also accepting our love obligations and our giftedness to fulfill those obligations.

HONESTY ABOUT AUTONOMY

But perhaps the most crucial area of denial we must expose is our denial about our autonomous independence—our dogged determination to make it in life without depending on God alone. This fist in the face of God may be very subtle, but God gets the message. I'm not given to rages or tantrums; my fist against God is a self-protective internal retreat from people, a refusal to engage others deeply or honestly so I won't have to depend on God to walk with me through my pain, anger, and loneliness.

A friend told me not long ago that I do battle against God and others quietly. She was right, but the quietness doesn't negate the wickedness of the battle. Some people rebel with promiscuity or substance abuse or blatant lawbreaking, but I try to make my life work without God by being super-religious, committed to impressing people with my godliness and wisdom. Quiet fists are no less rebellious than noisy ones. In God's eyes fists are fists, and unless we acknowledge and repent of our determined spirit of autonomy, our hearts will harden to His call and our hands will be closed to His grace.

Living by grace doesn't mean trying to purify our motives or asking God to give us pure motives. Motives are beyond our conscious control. God calls us to simply acknowledge the utter impurity of all our motives—none of us loves unconditionally. Our rebellion is worse than anybody thinks, worse than we ourselves think, so we can stop trying to clean up our lives; the fact is, we *can't* clean up our lives enough to earn God's acceptance. But we *can* receive His gracious forgiveness for the clenched fist we brandish at Him, and that forgiveness is the basis for accepting ourselves and offering grace to others.

BEFORE GOD, SELF, AND OTHERS

Denial is the enemy of intimacy. When we take moral inventory, we open ourselves to genuine relationship with God if our hearts are moved to repentance and confession. The psalmist records the disastrous results of his attempted denial and the rich response of God to his confessed sin:

> When I kept silent,
>   my bones wasted away
>   through my groaning all day long.
> For day and night
>   your hand was heavy upon me;
> my strength was sapped
>   as in the heat of summer.
> Then I acknowledged my sin to you
>   and did not cover up my iniquity.
> I said, "I will confess
>   my transgressions to the LORD"—
> and you forgave
>   the guilt of my sin. (Psalm 32:3-5)

When we stop denying our sin, our receiving of God's grace available through the Cross reconnects us with God's mercy and fellowship.

But we are also encouraged to confess our sins to others. James instructed, "Confess your sins to each other and pray for each other so that you may be healed" (James 5:16). Bill and I used to play both the pretend game and the blame game. When confronted with our weaknesses or failures to love, we either pretended they weren't that bad (minimizing or justifying our behavior) or blamed each other for what went wrong. One of the sweetest aspects of our present mutual interdependence is our willingness to simply admit the radical fallenness of our souls. We both long to bless and not harm, yet we know we are deeply flawed and unable to *not* hurt each other. The sweetness, however, is that we have found grace to not pretend but to acknowledge our betrayal, to not blame but to grieve our inevitable wounding of one another. Bill's sorrow—even tears—when he sees how he has damaged me reaches deep into my soul and makes me know I am loved well by a man of rich integrity.

The principle is expressed in Step Five of AA's Twelve-Step program, which says that we "*admitted to God, to ourselves, and to another human being the exact nature of our wrongs.*" Generic confession won't do. We must talk honestly about exactly what we did to wrong (i.e., fail to love) others, including God and ourselves. Verbalizing our specific sins against God, self, and others keeps us from slipping back into denial and moving forward into recovery.

Something important happens when we stop pretending we're better than we are. I always needed to believe I was better than others, sabotaging genuine friendship time and again in favor of self-protective piety. I'm still afraid to admit my sinfulness, thinking my perfection, if I could ever achieve it, would win others' approval.

Fortunately, however, experience is showing me that confession is good not only for the soul but for relationships as well. My friends seem to enjoy me as a human being instead of a "paragon of virtue." Bill and Christopher seem relieved—even glad—when I make and admit mistakes. Even I am beginning to like not having to be perfect.

One of the most powerful aspects of support groups like AA or Al Anon is the vulnerability they encourage. It's refreshing to drop our pretense and admit the pain and mistakes we encounter in recovery. How wonderful if believers could more openly acknowledge to one another their honest struggles concerning life and faith, seeking help and finding not condemnation but acceptance and encouragement! If we the forgiven cannot offer openness and forgiveness to fellow strugglers, we have missed our calling as ambassadors of Jesus' love.

EVIDENCE OF REPENTANCE

It's not enough just to admit our wrongs to ourselves, God, and some other person. The purpose of our moral inventory is not self-contempt (hating ourselves) or self-improvement (perfecting ourselves) but genuine repentance and the receiving of grace. Grace pursues us relentlessly, drawing us back again and again to feel the Father's strong arms around us and to experience His tears at our waywardness. Grace woos us from sin and makes us willing to live out our sorrow for sin by turning from it.

The first phase of repentance that is really lived out in our lives is expressed in AA's Step Six, which says we *"were entirely ready to have God remove all these defects of character"* exposed in the fourth step of our moral inventory. It won't be easy. Our inner pull toward self-sufficiency and lovelessness is reinforced by years of bad habits and a strong inclination toward rebellion and unbelief. We're used to our own way of doing things and don't want to learn to live in utter dependence on God. Said another way, we love our sin and don't want to give it up.

If we wait until we hate our sin, however, we may never let it go. But if we are *willing* to hate it more and more (because we see how it harms God, ourselves, and others), then God's Spirit will wean us from our character defects and salt our thirst for His grace. When we're ready to release our wrong designs for living, God will grace us to live without them.

God's strategy for weaning us from our death-bound attachments may seem harsh, even cruel. He is a jealous God, unwilling to share His beloved with any suitor promising (but unable to deliver) life. Sometimes He simply makes it clear the competition can't compete with His own strong love. In my own life God pulled out every prop supporting my life to show me I could depend on nothing except Him. I thought I would die when He put His hand on everything I held dear—my place in the church, my marriage, my status as a Bible teacher, my son's future, my financial security, my work as a writer, my friendships. But I didn't die. Instead, I found Him strong on my behalf and unfailingly faithful in His love. There was life in Him as He promised, and at times His presence was sweet beyond the bearing of it.

Nothing can compete with the kind of love God demonstrates toward us, but I don't experience that unless I relinquish—one day at a time, over and over again—my grasp on whatever false attachments and character flaws prevent me from loving Him and loving others with His love.

THROUGH GOD'S FORGIVENESS AND HELP

Coming out of denial about our longings, losses, pretense, and autonomy must eventually bring us to the final step in repentance: turning from our sin. Step Seven declares that we approached God and "*humbly asked him to remove our shortcomings.*"

What is lacking in the wording of this step—and it is a significant omission from a biblical perspective—is the basis on which we can ask God for anything, particularly the removal of our shortcomings (i.e., sins). Scripture explains that "without the shedding of blood there is no forgiveness" (Hebrews 9:22), and "Christ was sacrificed . . . to take away the sins of many people" (verse 28). Removal of our shortcomings is made possible by receiving Jesus Christ's sacrifice as payment for our sins. In fact, Christ's atonement is the only basis on which we can ask God for His grace to remove our shortcomings and escape our codependency. God removes our shortcomings in two senses. Let me explain.

First, He removes our sin judicially, granting us forgiveness because of our faith in Jesus' satisfaction of the death penalty we deserved for our sin. The theological term is *justification*, and it refers to our judicial standing as "not guilty" for our sin because the judgment fell on Jesus, not us.

But God also removes sin from our lives, helping us through His Spirit to stop doing what we shouldn't do and increasingly do what we ought to do. The theological word for this is *sanctification*, which refers to the changes we make to love with a more Christlike love, not so that He will love us but because He already does.

A key word in Step Seven is the word *humbly*. When we petition the Father to do His work of justification and sanctification in us, we must approach Him without demandingness, recognizing He owes us nothing and we owe Him everything. It is when we realize this that grace becomes most precious and we are moved to deep gratitude, overwhelmed that sinful as we are, yet "the LORD longs to be gracious to [us]; he rises to show [us] compassion" (Isaiah 30:18). Our power to turn from addiction and codependency comes finally not from fear of God's wrath but from fear of wounding the One we love by giving even a fraction of our heart's devotion to someone or something besides Him.

SUMMING UP

As we walk the road toward increasing interdependence in our relationships, we must continually work at renouncing our deep-seated patterns of self-deception. This will mean embracing our God-given longings, grieving the anger and sadness of our past and present losses, taking courageous inventory of our defects and giftedness, and repenting our recurring determination to live without God (however that may exhibit itself). When we stop pretending we're better than we are and abandon our attempts at impression management, we become ready for the changes God wants to accomplish in our lives. He will remove our shortcomings, both judicially (justifying us through Christ's atoning death) and experientially (sanctifying us through the Spirit's ongoing work in us), if we humbly ask Him to do so. And that will open the door to loving others without demandingness—the subject of the next chapter.

QUESTIONS FOR BUILDING COMMUNITY

1. Under what circumstances might "working the Twelve Steps" be a hindrance instead of an aid to recovery?
2. Name specific withdrawal symptoms of recovery from codependency.
3. What stands in the way of abandoning denial about our longings? Our losses? Our pretense? Our autonomy?
4. Why is it essential that our moral inventory include giftedness as well as character defects? Why is this hard for codependents?
5. How does your own autonomous independence evidence itself?
6. How does denial block intimacy? How does confession enhance intimacy?
7. What "supporting props" in your life did God pull out to bring you out of denial about your codependency?
8. How is God's removal of our character flaws a work of justification? Of sanctification?

NOTES
1. David A. Seamands, *Healing Grace* (Wheaton, IL: Scripture Press Publications, 1988), page 121.
2. Timmen Cermak, *A Time to Heal* (Los Angeles, CA: Jeremy P. Tarcher, Inc., 1988), page 161.

16

MUTUAL FREEDOM:
FREE TO RELINQUISH CONTROL

🍅

*It seems to me that free will is given to us for a purpose: so
that we may choose freely, without coercion or manipulation,
to love God in return, and to love one another in a similarly
perfect way. This is the deepest desire of our hearts.*
GERALD G. MAY
Addiction and Grace

One of the most essential ingredients of intimate relationships is
mutual freedom. Much as two people *desire* that the other change
into what they would like or give them the approval they long for,
both must be willing to give up the *demand* that those things happen.
The difference is subtle but profound.

The freedom that moves us toward intimacy is not merely freedom
from but freedom *to*—freedom from our codependent compulsion with
its concomitant fear and loneliness, and freedom to love without control and manipulation, to offer ourselves and receive others in mutual
interdependence.

BASIS FOR FREEDOM

Communion with God is what makes freedom possible. The Father frees
us to be who we are by loving us just as we are, and we are changed by
His grace. He thus models how we are to offer grace and at the same
time enables us to do so through His Spirit.

I remember the day I realized I no longer loved Bill. He'd hurt
me in ways I thought I could never forgive, and we had both run out

of reasons to love one another. I was watching him work out with his weights on the patio and wondering to myself, "How can I go on living with a man I don't love? I've seen the worst there is to see in him and I don't think he'll ever change. What am I going to do?"

Suddenly a question struck me with unexpected impact: *"Can God see what I see in Bill and still love this man?"*

It was a turning point for me. Of course God loved this man—as much as He loved this man's wife. It required no more effort for Him to accept Bill than to accept me. We both stood in desperate need of grace.

That realization marked the beginning of my accepting Bill just as he was, not because I found more to love in him, but because I found a resource beyond myself for loving him at his worst. When I asked God to give me His own love for Bill, an amazing grace entered my life and provided me with a strong bondedness toward my husband utterly beyond my own limited capacity. There was no rush of affection, but I knew without a doubt I would act on behalf of this man's good, offering him God's confrontation and His grace without hypocrisy.

The Father's unfailing love for Bill kept me persevering in the marriage until God eventually redeemed it in a wonderful way. I am convinced we connect ourselves to God's work in this world when we do what He came to do: *offer others freedom by confronting and accepting them just as they are for Jesus' sake, with the intention of inviting them into repentance and grace.*

REVOKING DEMANDINGNESS

Freedom is perhaps the most precious gift we offer another human being. Like charity, it must begin at home, as we offer *ourselves* the freedom to be ourselves. Because of God's acceptance we can let go of impression management and start just *living*. We can stop obligating and being obligated in our relationships. We can live unpretentiously because we know we are precious to God, and no one else's rejection has power to destroy us. We can gift ourselves with freedom.

And then we can gift others with a similar freedom—to be who they are without trying to make them change. We will long for them to become more Christlike and we'll confront them when they're not, but we won't take responsibility for making it happen. For many years I desperately wanted Bill to face his destructive drinking patterns; my goal was to get him into counseling or AA or both. My tactics changed from month to month, week to week, sometimes hour to hour. I might be sweet or angry, subtle or blatant. "Your drinking last night frightened [or angered or disgusted] me." Or, "I know you want to lose weight; do you know how many calories are in a can of beer?" Or perhaps, "Christopher wants to know if you're an alcoholic." Or maybe even, "I just heard about a new Christian counselor who's supposed to be really good." The strategies differed, but the demand was always the same: "You'd better conform to my expectations!"

Revoking my demandingness toward Bill was a lengthy and painful process. I never stopped desiring that he deal with his drinking patterns, but I learned to let go of trying to control him. For months I practiced stifling my comments, asking God to release me from my compulsion to manage Bill's life, and abandoning my control strategies, one at a time. Finally the time came when I no longer *had* to have Bill "behave" in order to be at peace within myself. Though I'd done my "homework," in the final analysis my letting go was a gift from the Father's hand, a serenity *He* worked in my soul.

Now it's Bill's turn. He desperately wants to change some things in me, particularly my frustrating habit of leaving piles of "stuff" around the house—five days' unexamined mail addressed to me, a quilting project I'm in the middle of, several articles from last week's newspaper I still want to read, coupons I have yet to cut out, clothes that need mending, etc., etc.—to say nothing of the chaos in my at-home office when I'm in the throes of completing a manuscript.

Bill has tried to control my inclination to slovenliness in many ways. The other night he said, "Honey [Why do I always get nervous when he calls me 'Honey' like that?], I'm not saying this in anger or anything, but I just counted thirteen piles of your stuff in the living room and dining room."

I suppressed my urge to go count them myself and justify what I found. But later as we talked, it became clear that the fact he'd actually *counted* my mounds of debris showed he was angry about it (despite his kind words) and was demanding that I change. Surely Bill need not give up his desire for neatness (and I must deal with the control and revenge issues on my side of that fence). But he will have to face his demandingness that I conform to his expectations. Learning to offer genuine freedom is a whole lot harder than it sounds.

ASPECTS OF FREEDOM

What does it mean to offer ourselves and others the freedom to love? As we work toward letting go of our codependent strategies for living, what will we become free to do or to be? Consider this partial list.

Free to Have Feelings
It seems strange to declare our right to have feelings, because feelings are one thing we cannot help but have. Our emotional responses to the events of our lives come unbidden, though we do have choices about whether or not to pay attention to them. Yet for many codependents, certain emotions were "forbidden" in childhood. No one ever told me, "You may not be angry." But I knew anger was dangerous, and I learned not to acknowledge or express my angry feelings.

Because of our childhood rules of silence, we as recovering codependents must occasionally remind ourselves that we are free to have all kinds of feelings. In fact, once we own and feel them, they no longer have the power to control or destroy us. And we have the Holy Spirit to give us wisdom in choosing what to do with them—to express them to anyone besides God, to act on them or not, and so on.

We must free others to have their own feelings, too, even when they make us uncomfortable or afraid. We must no longer judge them for their feelings, though we might insist they express them nondestructively. I still hate it when Bill is angry, but I can let him work it out if he's not hurting anyone with it. And he's learning to let me be preoccupied or sad without having to "fix" me or make me happy. Freedom to have feelings offers us a new lease on our emotional life, and it feels good.

Free to Have Needs
Another important freedom for recovering codependents is the right to have needs (emotional, physical, or spiritual) and to ask others to meet them. It's not true that everyone's needs but our own are valid. When we deny our neediness, we intensify our self-sufficiency toward God and shut ourselves off from mutual interdependence with people. It's repentance for codependents to acknowledge their needs and to ask God and others for help.

Freedom to have needs might mean seeing a doctor when our bodies don't feel right, or going to a counselor when we're having difficulty coping, or admitting to spiritual doubts and asking for prayer support. Or it may be as ordinary as requesting a teenage child to play the radio someplace else or not at all, or turning to a spouse or friend and saying, "I need a hug." It will feel demanding; having needs at all feels demanding to a codependent. But asking is not demanding unless we somehow get even when others fail to meet our needs.

We must let others have needs, too, and not feel guilty if we can't meet them all. In my more codependent days I saw myself as the great guru who could (and *should*) solve everyone's problems. It was progress for me the December I invited a friend to help decorate our Christmas tree and didn't try to counsel her. I just enjoyed our work of creating a thing of beauty without trying to "fix" or impress her. The experience ministered to both of us.

Free to Be Imperfect

Pia Mellody was right when she wrote, "It's the nature of a human being to be imperfect."[1] God certainly is a Holy God who unequivocally calls us as His redeemed children to holiness. Paul declared that God "saved us and called us to a holy life" (2 Timothy 1:9). However, that call to holy living doesn't mean we're perfectible in this life. In fact, the purpose of grace is not to make us perfect but to show us our need for a Savior, then show us the Savior we need, then create in us a burning desire to be more like Him. Jesus' life in us will become evident as we open ourselves to His grace, but in this life our fallenness is interwoven with our humanness, and we'll be imperfect until we're Home.

It's a reality I often forget. But increasingly I can acknowledge I'm sometimes wrong, often unloving, almost always self-concerned. I'm not glad of it nor content that it be so. I have a holy dissatisfaction with my character flaws. And Jesus' consuming love is burning off my dross. But I struggle less often to prove I'm right and even allow myself to be misunderstood once in a while. I'm worse than most people think, so I can let stand others' perception of me as imperfect.

I'm also learning to offer others freedom to be imperfect. I hurt when someone disappoints me, but I know I won't die and I don't have to leave the relationship because of it. And it takes a load off their shoulders to not *have* to meet my expectations. For years obligating others to love me shut me off from gladly receiving their freely chosen response to who I was.

Free to Deal with My Imperfection

A word of caution: Freedom to be imperfect doesn't excuse us from dealing with our imperfections. When we wrong others, we must repent and change. Steps Eight through Ten of AA's Twelve-Step recovery process are about clearing unbalanced accounts with others.

We begin by owning the sins of our past. Step Eight says we *"made a list of all persons we had harmed, and became willing to make amends to them all."* Our catalogs of love failures must be specific, naming both the persons and our sin against those persons. We must unflinchingly accept our guilt for having treated them badly. Making amends doesn't mean we do penance to compensate for the damage done through our irresponsibility or malice. But we must become willing to acknowledge our wrongs and seek the forgiveness of those we failed to love.

Free to Risk

Freedom from codependent bondage also allows for appropriate risk-taking in relationships. It doesn't mean allowing people to abuse us; in fact, we will feel more at risk when we let people be good to us (kindness in the past may have obligated us in ways we didn't like). Taking risks does mean refusing to control how others treat us and simply being ourselves, waiting to find out how they will react. Sometimes we'll be hurt, and sometimes we'll be incredibly blessed. Either way it's a risk we must take in order to be truly alive.

A good place to practice risking is in a support group of people traveling the same road to recovery. Not only will they be more likely than our family and friends to empathize with our pain, but they'll also be more apt to confront us with our wrong strategies. Their experience with recovery can teach us not to risk foolishly. The healthier we get, the more we'll be able to trust our own instincts.

Again the freedom must be two-way. We must also allow others freedom to risk. Instead of making it "safe," we can let others choose to act without assuring them of our positive reaction beforehand. Sometimes I don't like what my friends or family members do and I say so, but we're surviving my honesty without losing our love for each other. Sometimes they get hurt, but their risking has been good for our relationship.

One of our greatest risks will be approaching people we've failed to love, asking their forgiveness and seeking their good. AA's Step Nine says we "*made direct amends to [people we had harmed] wherever possible, except when to do so would injure them or others.*" Again, there is a fundamental danger in the concept of "making amends," as though we could somehow atone for our wrongs through what we might do or say. Grace, not compensation, must be the foundation of our restoration process. Making amends is not penance but repentance—asking forgiveness with an acknowledgment of our wrong and a commitment to change. The keys to risking wisely are our desire for restoration in the relationship and our commitment to the good of everyone involved. Clearing our own conscience is less the goal than blessing the other person with our repentance. When "making amends" merely reopens old wounds or is abusive to anyone, it is best to simply repent before God.

Free to Make Responsible Choices

Because codependents try to control people and circumstances, their newfound freedom to make responsible choices has two aspects to it. In recovery we acknowledge there are some things we can't change or control, while other things are definitely our responsibility and no one else's. Usually we confuse the two. The serenity prayer petitions, "God grant me the serenity to accept the things I cannot change, courage to change the things I can, and wisdom to know the difference." For most of us, wisdom is the hardest.

Simply stated, we ought to take responsibility for our own growth, attitudes, and behavior, and then give God control over everything else. We can't control our feelings, but we can face them and decide how or whether to express them (we *can* control how we act). Instead of blaming others for our emotions or choices, we can own them as ours, involving ourselves with fellow believers whose wisdom and maturity we trust, and asking God's Spirit to show us what we must do and when. God is faithful to show His will to any who humbly seek it and are willing to obey it.

We also must give others freedom over their actions. We can stop being caretakers and let others do what they can do for themselves. We can stop rescuing others, refusing to interfere with the natural consequences of their choices. It will feel unloving, even cruel, to hold others accountable for their own lives and emotions, but it is deeply respectful of their dignity and personhood and is therefore truly loving. Instead of frantically praying, "Lord, make this person stop drinking (or cheating or overworking, etc.)," we can simply ask, "Lord, draw me close enough to Yourself so that I can release this one I love until You bring him to the end of himself so he, too, will seek You."

This appropriate "division of responsibility" (each person responsible only for himself or herself) is an ongoing process that keeps short accounts with God, self, and others. AA's Step Ten declares that we "*continued to take personal inventory, and when we were wrong promptly admitted it.*" Humility and willingness to repent and ask forgiveness must become a way of life, not just a once-and-for-all event. We need take responsibility only for our own wrongs and not mind anyone else's business, daily seeking forgiveness on the three levels described by David Seamands: *active* forgiveness (forgiving others the wrong they've done to us); *passive* forgiveness (receiving forgiveness for the wrong we've done); and *reflective* forgiveness (forgiving ourselves for our imperfections).[2] Living responsibly is not easy, but it is incredibly freeing.

Free to Be Spontaneous

One final freedom experienced by recovering codependents is the freedom to be spontaneous—i.e., to enter the unknown without self-protection. Spontaneity can't be programed or controlled; as soon as we try to make it happen, we keep it from happening. But as our life becomes less self-centered and more other-directed, our self-consciousness will gradually fade, and we'll eventually be surprised to realize we're paying less attention to how others are perceiving us and more attention to how we're blessing them. Our journey out of codependency proceeds imperceptibly, one experience at a time away from enmeshment and into the freedom of mutual interdependence. One day our spontaneity will simply be a part of who we are.

In the meantime, we must also allow others the freedom of spontaneity. Instead of demanding "no surprises," we can stop trying to predict what others will do or say and simply wait and see. It will feel like death; as codependents we used our sensitivity to others' thoughts and feelings as a safety belt protecting us from sudden direction-changes in relationships. When we let go of controlling others and just take care of our own "stuff," everything will be in turmoil for a time because the rules in the relationship will have changed. Old inclinations to control or obsess persist despite our best intentions. But we can accept the reality that if we're going to live in grace we're going to live with pain, and over time the pain will frighten us less and less.

In my own marriage the turmoil lasted almost four years; for others it may last even longer. It was hard to choose time and again to let go of my attempts to control Bill. Eventually the letting go was a gift God gave, an inner serenity regarding the addiction I wanted to change in him. And now that Bill has joined me on the journey out of codependency, he, too, has entered the process of letting go of what he wants changed in me.

The other day at breakfast I asked Bill, "What do you experience as different in the way I love you now, compared to how I loved you ten years ago?" In the discussion that followed, he said he no longer senses in me any expectation of him except that he be himself and be honest. He went on to say that for many years I'd had subtle demands about his performance in many areas, demands that put terrible pressure on him. Believing he couldn't be the loving, strong, spiritual leader I wanted, he never dared look into my eyes or into my soul, nor would he let me look into his soul for fear I'd see his inadequacy. My giving up those demands and Bill's increasing dependency on God is changing that fear, and it's making a wonderful difference in our relationship. Bill said he is now able to look into his own soul, admit and grieve over his weaknesses, and then offer his real self to me, knowing I have weaknesses as well and can accept him without forcing him into my mold. That morning talk brought deep joy to both of us.

The long-term rewards of the freedom Bill and I enjoy have been more than worth the agony of the process we had to go through. Hard as it was, we wouldn't trade the relationship we have now for any amount of supposed control we might exercise over one another. Spontaneity is just too much fun.

SUMMING UP

Mutual freedom is integral to the survival of any relationship. God offers it to us as His created image-bearers, and He calls us to offer it to ourselves and to others in the same way. Freedom from codependency means we can be and let be, live and let live, without trying to manage anyone's business but our own. It will be hard. It will seem unnatural. It will cause us pain. But it will make us alive if in the process we learn to depend utterly on God. That is the focus of the next chapter.

QUESTIONS FOR BUILDING COMMUNITY

1. Name some codependent behaviors you or someone you know well have done that violated others' freedom.
2. Why is freedom essential to intimacy?
3. Tell how the following ways to deal with unwelcome feelings are biblical or unbiblical:
   a. Pretend you don't feel them.
   b. Lie to others about having them.
   c. Tell others just what you feel when you feel it.
   d. Tell others what you feel only if it won't upset them.
   e. Tell what you're feeling if it's for the other person's good.
   f. Tell God exactly what you're feeling—about Him and others.
4. What kind of freedom is hardest for you? Why?
   a. To have feelings
   b. To have needs
   c. To be imperfect
   d. To deal with imperfections
   e. To risk
   f. To make good choices
   g. To be spontaneous
5. How might it be either codependent *or* healthy to ask for what we need?
6. What's the difference between accepting our imperfections and ignoring our sin?
7. If you were spontaneous, what would that look like?
8. What are the dangers of offering others freedom?

NOTES
1. Pia Mellody, Andrea Wells Miller, and J. Keith Miller, *Facing Codependence* (San Francisco, CA: Harper & Row, Publishers, 1989), page 66.
2. David A. Seamands, *Healing Grace* (Wheaton, IL: Scripture Press Publications, 1988), pages 163-164.

17

SPIRITUAL VITALITY: FREE TO TRUST AND OBEY

❦

*Ultimately, our yearning for God is the most important
aspect of our humanity, our most precious treasure;
it gives our existence meaning and direction.*
GERALD G. MAY
Addiction and Grace

"One-three-eleven, one-three-eleven—that's the key!" Ann, my Al-Anon friend, was referring to the spiritual emphasis of AA's Twelve-Step program. Step One exposes our helplessness to manage our lives, Step Three stresses God's care as we turn our lives and wills over to Him, and Step Eleven deals with our ongoing connectedness and obedience to God. "One-three-eleven" summarizes the program's focus on spirituality in the recovery process for codependents.

Step Eleven declares that as recovering codependents we *"sought through prayer and meditation to improve our conscious contact with God as we understood him, praying only for knowledge of his will for us and the power to carry that out."* Let's examine that commitment to God-connectedness and what it promises to those who pursue it.

SEEKERS OF THE KING

The word *sought* presupposes a fervent desire for something lacking and implies a pursuit after one's deepest longings. Because we were made for relationship with God, our yearning after Him should not surprise us. When we stop running from Him and acknowledge that His love is what we deeply want after all, our seeking will be rewarded by His coming to us.

Moses warned the Israelites just before entering the Promised Land that if they someday turned from God, He would scatter them among the pagan nations to bring them to their senses. Then Moses added this promise: "If from there you seek the LORD your God, you will find him if you look for him with all your heart and with all your soul" (Deuteronomy 4:29). Jesus said, "Everyone who . . . seeks finds" (Matthew 7:8). God's heart leans toward those whose hearts yearn for Him. If we hunger after God for our very life, we are never disappointed.

THROUGH PRAYER AND MEDITATION

Prayer and meditation are distasteful, almost repulsive, to the contemporary mentality. It's not just that we're too busy to quiet our hearts in unhurried conversation with God. Rather, prayer and meditation say something about us we're loathe to admit.

Prayer says we're dependent creatures responsible to ask for what we cannot provide ourselves. We seldom pray (except by habit) unless we sense our own helplessness in a situation. Our family recently experienced the death by cancer of Bill's stepfather, and the process was excruciating. There's something about the inevitability and finality of death that reminds us of our utter inability to control our own lives. Our helplessness in the face of death forces us into dependence on God. Prayer (communicating with God) puts to death our insistence on "doing it my way." And meditation (spending time thinking God's thoughts as they apply to our lives) forces us to wait on God for His direction instead of acting impulsively in our own self-interest.

Prayer and meditation in and of themselves will not necessarily usher us into God's presence nor communicate His grace to us. Grace doesn't respond to formulas—no pushing the right button and demanding that God deliver on His promises. But unless we quiet our spirits in a posture of asking and receiving, we can't sustain the relationship with Him that brings us life. We must fervently desire His grace and His will before we can receive either. That's why prayer and meditation are vitally important to the recovery process for repentant codependents.

BONDING WITH GOD

Our commitment in Step Eleven "to improve our conscious contact with God" is the cornerstone of AA's Twelve-Step recovery program. Donald Joy has said, "All humans are bonding beings, such that their yearning for intimacy is an internal magnet which draws them, often unwittingly, toward God, for whose intimate relationship they are created."[1] *Improving our contact with God is life's most important objective, giving meaning to our lives and enabling us to love Him and others with boldness and passion.*

At a recent recovery conference I spoke with a young man who had been abused and abandoned by his mother, herself an alcoholic with a traumatized childhood. He said he had confronted her with the impact of that loss in his life, and she had responded by asking, "How could I give you something I never received?"

It is a profound question. The truth is, we cannot give what we have not received. That is why we desperately need God's gift of bonding. Just as an infant needs his parents to bond with him quite apart from anything the infant has done or can do for them, so we need God to bond with us simply because He loves us. We can't give love away unless we've received it from God.

God bonds with us, His children, in three ways: He offers us His love, He longs for our love, and He allows us to impact Him.

Of all God's blessings, the most wondrous is His gift of love. The Apostle John wrote, "This is love: not that we loved God, but that he loved us and sent his Son as an atoning sacrifice for our sins" (1 John 4:10). God moved to bond with us at the cost of His Son's death on our behalf. There's never been a love to equal that.

All parents desire their children's love in return for theirs. Our heavenly Father is no exception. "Love the LORD your God with all your heart and with all your soul and with all your strength," Moses instructed the Israelites (Deuteronomy 6:5). God cares about our response to Him; adequate bonding requires reciprocal love.

The corollary to God's longing for our heart-response to Him is that He allows us to have impact on Him. What we do or feel *matters* to God. The Apostle Paul instructed us to live righteous lives of genuine love for others and warned us not to "grieve the Holy Spirit of God" (Ephesians 4:30). Our sin wounds the heart of God, and He grieves over the wrong choices of His beloved children. I often think of my Father's tears when I misuse His gifts or turn back to my former idols of control and self-sufficiency. Jesus also taught that "there is rejoicing in the presence of the angels of God over one sinner who repents" (Luke 15:10), and I sometimes imagine God Himself smiling or holding out His arms to me when I repent of a sin He has shown me. Our relational choices call forth God's involved response, just as our confusion and weakness call forth His fervent intercession on our behalf: "The Spirit helps us in our weakness. We do not know what we ought to pray for, but the Spirit himself intercedes for us with groans that words cannot express" (Romans 8:26). How amazing that the God of the universe cares for me with such a steady and impassioned love! "Even when our choices are destructive and their consequences hurtful, God's love remains unwavering. . . . [He] is constantly open and vulnerable to us."[2]

PRAYING FOR KNOWLEDGE OF GOD'S WILL

Though none of us escapes the rebellion and self-centeredness resulting from the Fall, loved children generally seek to please and be pleasing to their parents. Likewise, our redeemed nature as beloved children of God draws us toward obedience. "If you love me," Jesus said, "you will obey what I command" (John 14:15). The first question in the Heidelberg Catechism, a beautiful sixteenth-century Reformation treatise, asks, "What is your only comfort in life and in death?" The answer is: "That I am not my own, but belong—body and soul, in life and in death—to my faithful Savior Jesus Christ. . . . Because I belong to him, Christ, by his Holy Spirit, assures me of eternal life and makes me whole-heartedly willing and ready from now on to live for him."[3]

When we know we belong to Someone who loves us, we want to please the One to whom we belong. According to AA's Step Eleven, in recovery we pray *only for knowledge of [God's] will for us.* "Only" suggests the high priority we should set on discovering and doing what God wants us to do. When we realize we've been created and loved in order to bring Him glory, our most important work is to find out how to do so.

What *is* God's will for us? AA's eleventh step implies it's a daily quest to discover what He wants us to do in any given moment. In some ways that is true. Obedience to God's will may be different for different people. My repentance in turning from my love failure may come through in one way and Bill's in another because our particular styles of self-protective lovelessness are not alike. There are also questions of timing and method involved; I may need to confront a friend or family member on a particular issue, but *when* and *how* I do so will determine whether I am genuinely obeying God's command to love others as myself. For that I need the Holy Spirit's individual witness to my spirit.

However, there are some scriptural aspects of God's will that seem especially relevant to recovering codependents. Let's take a look at just three.

God Wants Us to Worship

"Man's chief end," according to the Westminster Shorter Catechism, "is to glorify God, and to enjoy him forever."[4] Doing God's will involves honoring and worshiping Him, not just in church but in every phase of our living. Worship means acknowledging God as God and quieting our spirits in reverence before Him.

"The worship of God is nowhere defined in Scripture," wrote W. E. Vine. "Broadly it may be regarded as the direct acknowledgement to God, of His nature, attributes, ways and claims."[5] Contrary to rebellious autonomy, the worshiping heart lets God be God and accepts itself as under His care and authority. In worship we accept God's will (particularly in those circumstances we'd most like to change) even when we don't understand it, don't like it, and wouldn't have chosen it. Jesus worshiped in Gethsemane when He conceded, "My Father, if it is not possible for this cup to be taken away unless I drink it, may your will be done" (Matthew 26:42). We worship in our own Gethsemane when we submit our wills to God's.

In worship we sometimes accept literally the invitation of the psalmist: "Come, let us bow down in worship, let us kneel before the LORD our Maker" (Psalm 95:6-7). But even when we don't bend our knees, we can bend our hearts before God. It will take some effort. A. W. Tozer lamented the contemporary Christian's difficulty in quieting the inner man: "We have lost our spirit of worship and our ability to withdraw inwardly to meet God in adoring silence. . . . The words, 'Be still, and know that I am God,' mean next to nothing to the self-confident, bustling worshiper in this middle period of the twentieth century."[6] Yet, despite the discipline required to spend time adoring our Lord, we can take comfort in knowing we carry our own altar within and can worship anytime and anywhere we find a quiet moment in His presence. It is, after all, God's will that we worship Him.

God Wants Us to Believe

Jesus was once asked, "What must we do to do the works God requires?" (John 6:28). The question hinted at achieving status with God through the accomplishment of pious works. Jesus' answer was a surprise: "The work of God is this: to believe in the one he has sent" (verse 29).

If what God wants first from us is faith in His Son, Jesus, then we as codependents must rethink our former lifestyle. We've always been doers, accomplishers, goal-directed achievers; we've even tried hard to be spiritual. And here Jesus asks us simply to believe in Him in order to please the Father. It's something of a shock to learn that *the opposite of sin is not virtue but faith*, not doing good but trusting in Jesus' death on our behalf.

Let's not be confused. Jesus isn't asking us to stop our accomplishing or achieving. What were liabilities in our former codependent lifestyle can become assets as we redirect them into appropriate loving service of others. But in the realm of the spiritual, when we consider what we must do to please God, we must shift gears and remember that faith in Christ is both His gift to us (Ephesians 2:8) and also our return gift to Him. It is, in fact, all we have to recommend us to the Father.

Jesus calls us to live out our faith by finding our rest in Him. How unlike the hurried, often frenzied pace we codependents are accustomed to! We'd much rather be in charge, self-sufficient, controlling.

Not long ago my mother-in-law broke her hip at a time when everyone who could have helped her was unavailable except me. The hospital was over thirty miles away, and I was there every day to oversee her surgery, confer with her doctors, and see to her needs. As exhausting as the regimen was, it felt fulfilling, even noble, to be that needed. When others returned to help care for her, I was chagrined to realize that, though my care was a genuine expression of my love for her, I'd enjoyed my role as trauma-responder too much. It was even hard to let other people care for me as I reacted to the trauma *I* had been through. Resting doesn't come easily to recovering codependents.

Jesus had sorrow in His voice when He lamented that the people of

Jerusalem were not willing to have been gathered to Himself "as a hen gathers her chicks under her wings" (Matthew 23:37), a decidedly maternal gesture of comfort. We codependents would so much rather give than receive, wear ourselves out than ask for help. It is to us that Jesus' words seem most directed: "Come to me, all you who are weary and burdened, and I will give you rest. Take my yoke upon you and learn from me, for I am gentle and humble in heart, and you will find rest for your souls. For my yoke is easy and my burden is light" (Matthew 11:28-30). What a trade-off—my anxiety for His peace, my ill-fitting frenzy for His gentle guidance, my need to control for His offer of soul-rest.

We, as God's redeemed children, deeply want to please Him, yet we also hate to give up our familiar codependent strategies. We continually grapple with what we want more—to believe and rest only in Him or to hang on to our control or fear or anger. We make the choice a dozen or more times each day in big and little ways. In my own life God comes out second a lot. I so often would rather help, work, counsel, eat, expound, control—any of the things I do instead of facing my pain and living in lonely dependence on God in the moment. "Do you love me?" Jesus asks again and again. And time after time we give Him our answer—by choosing whether to stay safe through our own devices or risk facing our pain or inadequacy, resting in Him alone. It's never a simple choice. Yet even when we betray Him, His grace is available through our repentance.

God Wants Us to Love

When Jesus was asked to name the greatest of God's commandments, He replied, "'Love the Lord your God with all your heart and with all your soul and with all your mind.' This is the first and greatest commandment. And the second is like it: 'Love your neighbor as yourself'" (Matthew 22:37-39). Obedience to God's will must involve mutual interdependence with others. Our calling is to love not just God but our fellowman as well. The next chapter will deal with this commandment in greater detail.

PRAYING FOR POWER TO OBEY

The only encouragement I have that I am able to love as Jesus loved is that He has given me His Spirit to do in me what I cannot do by my own strength. Step Eleven specifically mentions praying for "the power to carry . . . out" God's will for us, and that power is available to believers through the Holy Spirit.

It is not a power we strive to obtain; we simply use what is already there. Jesus compared it to a branch being attached to a vine and bearing fruit (John 15:1-8). "Remain in me," Jesus said to His disciples, "and I will remain in you. No branch can bear fruit by itself; it must remain in the vine. Neither can you bear fruit unless you remain in me. . . . Apart from me you can do nothing" (John 15:4-5). Branches don't strain to produce grapes; grapes just *happen* because the branches they're growing on are connected to the source of nourishment. We can't generate the power to obey God's will. The power comes from staying in fellowship with God and doing what the Spirit tells us to do, facing the consequences of that obedience through the comfort He affords.

If we obey, we'll suffer. It won't be comfortable or convenient or popular for us to stop acting codependently, and all Jesus promised is His Spirit's presence to comfort us. Abiding in Jesus means acting like He acted, assured that He'll be there to sustain us in the aftermath of our right choices. Self-effort must give way to trusting surrender, self-protection exchanged for risking love, self-preoccupation yielded to other-centeredness. Allowing the indwelling Spirit of Jesus to direct our choices, and then just doing what He says, is all the power we need.

Often the Spirit tells us what to do and we don't listen. My friend Lisa knew she was taking on too much work, but she didn't want to disappoint her boss and fellow workers. Her consequent bleeding ulcer wasn't the result of ignorance or an inner Power shortage. Knowing *what* to do is seldom the problem; the hard thing is accepting the consequences of doing what's right. Being the office hero was more important to Lisa than protecting her health. Her codependency won that round, but the fight's not over and the Spirit won't leave her. She'll have another chance.

SUMMING UP

Even my wrong attachments (once I acknowledge and turn from them) work for my good by bringing me to a realization of my helplessness, God's grace, and the possibility of resting in a life-sustaining relationship with Him. Except for my debilitating codependency, I might never have seen the futility of living without God. As Gerald May has said, "If my attachments had not caused me to fail miserably at controlling my life and work, I doubt I ever would have recovered the spiritual desire and the sense of God that had been so precious to me as a child."[7]

Becoming and remaining connected to God our Father is life—spiritual vitality. It doesn't assure us a carefree existence or the elimination of problems. In fact, depending on Him alone often creates more problems than we had as practicing codependents. But knowing and doing what He wants means living as we were intended to live—vitally connected to and in tune with Him, bearing the spiritual fruit of passionate love for Him, ourselves, and others. Our love won't be perfect and we'll make a lot of mistakes along the way. But because we're connected to God through His Spirit living in us, we can move with boldness into the pain of loving as He loved us—the topic of the final chapter.

QUESTIONS FOR BUILDING COMMUNITY

1. At what point in your life did you become willing to seek God with your whole heart?
2. What did you do to seek Him? What was the result?
3. What most draws you to prayer and meditation? What most hinders you?
4. What frightens you about bonding with God? What blesses you?
5. If abuse and nonnurturing are passed from one generation to the next (because we can't give what we haven't received), how is it possible to break that destructive cycle?
6. What have you received from God that you've been able to offer to someone else? Be specific.
7. What particular things have you done this week that caused God either joy or sadness? How might you have more enjoyed His pleasure and/or grieved His sorrow?
8. Which aspect of God's will is hardest for you? Why?
   a. To believe
   b. To rest
   c. To love
9. In what specific way(s) do you "tap in" to God's power for your obedience?

NOTES

1. Donald M. Joy, *Bonding: Relationships in the Image of God* (Waco, TX: Word Books Publisher, 1985), page ix.
2. Gerald May, *Addiction and Grace* (San Francisco, CA: Harper & Row, Publishers, 1988), page 123.
3. *Psalter Hymnal* (Grand Rapids, MI: Publication Committee of the Christian Reformed Church, Inc., 1959), page 22 of the "Doctrinal Standards" section of the hymnal.
4. *The Westminster Standards* (Philadelphia, PA: Great Commission Publications), page 71.
5. W. E. Vine, *Vine's Expository Dictionary of Old and New Testament Words* (Old Tappan, NJ: Fleming H. Revell Company, 1981), volume 4, page 236.
6. A. W. Tozer, *The Knowledge of the Holy* (San Francisco, CA: Harper & Row, Publishers, 1961), page 6.
7. May, page 10.

18

SACRIFICIAL LOVE: FREE TO RISK AND SUFFER

❦

What we sometimes call "salvation" or "grace" is really
a grand scheme, by which all of life can be focused
on the one goal of the Creation: that humans may live fully
and intimately with other persons and with God.
DONALD JOY
Bonding: Relationships in the Image of God

The bondage of codependency keeps us believing and acting on lies (about ourselves, God, and others) that imprison our souls and prevent us from loving others and from being fully alive. We become slaves to our false beliefs and false selves, grieving the heart of God, who created us for freedom and intimacy. He calls us to risk moving from bondage to bonding.

Bonding is the love-connection we enjoy with God and others that motivates us to worship God as Sovereign Lord and to do for others whatever is for their ultimate well-being. Love (energy directed toward God's glory and another's good) must characterize who we are, not merely determine what we do.

Bonding with God and knowing we belong to Him is the basis for healing all losses and rebuilding all broken relationships. The focus of grace is always restoration to community—our true selves in loving relationship with others' true selves. The stronger our bond with God, the greater our capacity for mutual interdependence. Other-bonding is always God's intention: "Dear friends, since God so loved us, we also ought to love one another" (1 John 4:11).

AA's twelfth step affirms this commitment to God and others:

"Having had a spiritual awakening as the result of these Steps, we tried to carry this message to others, and to practice these principles in all our affairs." Our new spiritual vitality as recovering codependents so transforms us that we long to bless others with the hope we've discovered. David Seamands rightly challenges us:

> There are simply not enough professionally trained counselors to work with the growing numbers of damaged and hurting people. God wants to raise up a vast army of healed helpers whom He can use as His "temporary assistants to the Holy Spirit." This is the ultimate purpose of healing grace in your life—to turn you into a channel of healing grace in someone else's life.[1]

No matter how selfless we may appear to others and ourselves, we codependents have been adamantly committed to our own self-preservation. Preoccupied with our compulsive strategies for controlling our world, we haven't focused ultimately on anyone but ourselves. In recovery, our focus must take a radical shift—from self-preoccupation to other-centeredness. Even as we pursue the necessary process of dealing with our own woundedness, anger, and grief, we must never forget our congenital need for God's forgiving grace in our lives and His injunction to love others. We cannot hurry the process or skip over the pain. But our ultimate goal must be to get on with the primary reason for our being here: *to gratefully love God above all and to more selflessly love our neighbor as we increasingly value ourselves.* Let's explore what's involved in offering others the gift of bonding.

RECIPIENTS OF BONDING

Bonding is a strong word, conjuring up the kind of deep intimacy generally reserved for primary relationships—between parents and children, or between lovers, for example. But bonding in the present context refers to a recovering codependent's general openness to connect with others, though of course the connection won't be the same for everyone. There are different levels of bonding.

Parental Rebonding
Because the parent-child bond is crucial to our view of self, we long to "make peace" with our parents, whether they're living or not. To

the degree the parental bond was inadequate or lost in childhood we must acknowledge the anger and grief that accompanied its loss. Our longing for parental bonding doesn't diminish over the years; it goes on driving us in ways we may not even comprehend. Our emotional ambiguity regarding our parents cries out for resolution.

God's ultimate goal for His redeemed people is always restoration to relationship, but not just any kind of relationship. God calls us to imitate His own hearty love toward us, to charactertize our relationships by reciprocal good intentions based on mutual honesty and genuine repentance for past love failures. When those elements are present, we can move toward repairing and/or establishing bondedness with our parents.

Loving them God's way may mean confronting them with the nurturing losses that resulted from their addictions or abuse. This is terrifying for codependents, who avoid conflict and are avidly committed to protecting one or both parents. The primary objective is not restoration of the parent-child relationship for *our* sakes, but restoration of *their* unguarded relationship with God, whatever personal change and sacrifice that might demand of us. We are called to reflect God's bold, no-nonsense love toward our parents in a way that reveals their failure to have met our needs but doesn't destroy them in the process. Ultimately, our intention in confronting others about their sin should be to invite them to a level of repentance that can open them to a deeper communion with God than they could have enjoyed before.

It will take prayer and planning and wise honesty to learn to love our parents well. We will make mistakes because our human nature is not abrogated by our good intentions. But we are called to think, to pray, to risk, and to move with courage toward genuine forgiveness and a new, strong love for our parents that flows from our connectedness with God. Our efforts to love well may not "pay off" in a more intimate relationship with them. In fact, a lack of repentance on their part may prevent the restoration God longs for. But if we are to live out our own repentance, we must ask God to show us how to offer a right kind of love to our parents.

Bonding with a Spouse or Close Friend

Intimate relationships are always a matter of the heart. When addiction is present—to drugs, alcohol, work, infidelity, pornography, or

whatever—commitments of the heart are compromised, and both partners sense it in their spirits. A man whose wife is enmeshed in her
job as church secretary complained to me that she's too tired to spend
time with him anymore. She gives herself so wholeheartedly at work,
she has little interest or energy left for him. She's even become dis-
interested in the devotional time they used to have together. He's tried
to introduce their former activities back into their life, but his efforts
miss the mark. The sad truth is that he's no longer a priority to her.
She has closed her heart to him in opening it to the fulfillment of her
job, and nothing else—not renewed devotions nor time together nor
counseling—will satisfy unless she repents of her workaholism and
brings her heart back to him.

The addiction and/or codependency present in an intimate relationship must be addressed before genuine bonding can become reality.
A relationship is a delicate balancing act, and unaddressed addictions
upset the equilibrium. The change process is almost never even; usually
one person is ready to drop the wrong dependency long before the other.
In such cases, offering one's whole heart may need to be postponed until
the other is ready to receive it. Jesus told His disciples shortly before His
death, "I have much more to say to you, more than you can now bear"
(John 16:12). Perhaps because of their spiritual shallowness or because
the Holy Spirit hadn't yet been given, they had limits on the depth of
their intimacy with Jesus.

So also, we may discover limits in our relationships. Someone we
love deeply may be unable to hear the depth of our pain or to share the
burden of our self-discoveries. *We may need to suffer the loneliness of
a waiting love*, walking the tightrope of inviting the other in without
revictimizing ourselves. Finally, we may need to relinquish the dream
of deep intimacy with that person and turn to God with our overflow-
ing hearts.

Mutual interdependence is our deepest desire; it must be mutual
if it is to thrive as God intended. But especially in a committed relationship, God's love constrains us to go on doing what is good for the
other and what will keep us dependent on Him. In His own time and
way, God may bring healing to the friendship or marriage, particularly
if both partners are willing to be honest about their pain and their sin,
to repent of their lack of love, to lean utterly on God for His indwelling
Spirit, and to change their wrong habits, one day at a time.

Bonding with Friends and Acquaintances

The connecting we do with our more casual friends and acquaintances is different in degree from that which we pursue with our parents or closest companions. Not everyone can receive my heart or bear the weight of my soul. There are those who can receive only some of what I have to offer. Jesus touched the lives of hundreds of people through His teaching and healing. But He opened His heart to only a few—His parents, His disciples, and those close friends who were committed to His ministry.

Yet in all of Jesus' interactions with both friends and antagonists, Jesus offered His true self. He didn't pretend; He didn't put on airs; He didn't try to protect Himself. He just was who He was. And we can be the same. Even with those we don't know at all well, we can maintain an openness to just being ourselves, offering our acceptance of them as they are because we are in the habit of accepting ourselves as we are.

THE COST OF BONDING

If we are willing to pursue genuine bonding and Christlike love in the relationships God has given us, we will experience tremendous benefits. The possibility of greater personal wholeness, relational intimacy, and spiritual vitality is to be celebrated. But bonding also has a price. The cost of connectedness can be enormous, particularly in terms of risk-taking and suffering.

Willingness to Risk

Bonding can't develop without substantial risks of faith. Jesus commissioned His disciples just before His death, saying, "Love each other as I have loved you. Greater love has no one than this, that he lay down his life for his friends" (John 15:12-13). Within twenty-four hours He did Himself what He'd asked them to do: He laid down His life for them on the cross.

It's His will for us, too—to love others by giving up our lives for them. When we abandon our codependency, we abandon life as we've known it, and it will feel like death. I hate not being in charge; I want to know what's going to happen so I can control it. Letting others be who they are instead of fitting them into my mold is terrifying. I'm desperate to prevent conflict. I can't stand to be angry or to have others angry with me; I'm afraid I'll die if everyone isn't happy with me. Grace burns my self-sufficient soul, blistering my pride and consuming my comfortable haughtiness; it's not easy being loved unconditionally. I don't want Jesus mourning when I fail to stand for Him; I despise the responsibility.

What brings us into life always feels like death. And that's what God wills us to choose: *death to our comfortable self-centeredness and entry into the terror of grace.* Our illusions must die, and so must our demandingness that God and others "be there" for us. The blackness usually deepens as we enter life. In exchange for our codependency God offers us perplexity, pain, loneliness, and a lingering sorrow only Home will assuage. It is an agonizing passage, and one that is never over this side of Heaven, in spite of the rich joys we discover as we learn to love in new ways. In choosing life we must first choose death. That's what it means to love. Most days I don't even come close.

Risk implies danger of pain, and we have an aversion to pain. Yet the irony is that unless we risk being hurt, we can't know what it is to be loved. Like the velveteen rabbit in the tale by Margery Williams, we must have our fur loved off and become quite shabby if we're to be truly real and alive.[2] Risking doesn't get less dangerous the more we do it; Gerald May has said,

> Because real risking in faith can occur only in those areas
> of life where we feel most impoverished and vulnerable, it
> never becomes something we are really comfortable with. . . .
> Each choice remains difficult; what really becomes condi-
> tioned in this process is simply our willingness and readi-
> ness to *take* the risks of faith. They never stop feeling like
> risks.[3]

There's no way around it: *If I'm going to love and be loved, I'm going to be hurt and uncomfortable.* Only grace affords the courage necessary to take the risks.

Choosing to Suffer

If there's one thing codependents are good at, it's suffering. We pity ourselves for it and complain that we have no choice, but inwardly we pride ourselves in it. Suffering is a compulsion with us; we unconsciously seek out situations where we must give more than we receive, more even than we have to offer. We feel cheated if there's no pain or discomfort for us to endure. In the context of the abusive backgrounds from which we've emerged, the word for our suffering is *revictimization*. Often we do it to ourselves.

The suffering involved in appropriate bonding is another thing altogether. It comes not from a victimization compulsion but from a willingness to act in another person's best interest even if we must suffer for it. The difference is summarized in one word: *choice*.

Chosen suffering is not self-directed—trying to win approval, admiration, or sympathy for oneself by being in pain. Rather, it is other-directed—enduring patiently the pain that may come as the result of doing whatever is necessary to offer strong love to another human being. We must come full cycle from our bondage to the whims of others for our own sakes, to the freedom of choosing to suffer for the sake of others.

Jesus set the standard, *choosing* to leave Heaven and face the cross in order to live out His unfailing love toward His own. He wasn't a helpless victim, feeling unworthy of better treatment. Paul says Jesus knew Himself to be God but "did not consider equality with God something to be grasped" (Philippians 2:6). Instead, He "made himself nothing, taking the very nature of a servant" (verse 7)—something He chose to do to Himself. He operated from a position of inner, personal strength in His sacrificing. So can we.

This Christlike abrogation of our own comfort or convenience for the sake of doing constructive good for others is a powerful and productive kind of suffering. Its purpose is to draw others to Christ, not to draw attention to ourselves. We face the pain of standing ever ready to offer our hearts, not so we'll be loved, but because it is our redeemed nature to love selflessly as Jesus loved. His Spirit generates other-centeredness in us and keeps us doggedly committed to sacrificial living. Father John Shea wrote,

> Whenever people expend themselves, they want results. If they lay down life, they want someone's life raised up. If they empty themselves, they want someone to be filled. They want their sufferings to bear fruit. If this doesn't happen, they're tempted to give up. The refusal of the gift quickly becomes a reason not to

offer it. Instead of leaning into resistance with love, they'll back off and say, "Well, we tried."

However, the motive for offering love is not that it be successful. Christians want response, but they are not bound to it. They sacrifice for others because they are the recipients of sacrifice. They are the current generation of a long line of broken bodies and shed blood. This gift Christians have received, they freely give. They join the living history in enacting the dream of God, [which] is a people sustained and transformed by mutual sacrificial love.[4]

To the degree Christ is given a free hand to live through us, we will love sacrificially. It is our (new) nature.

FOR THE HOPE SET BEFORE US

Our Christlike chosen suffering is not just the result of others' failure to meet our need for love and involvement. Even when bonding with others offers us wonderful tastes of intimacy, we suffer because we're alive to our insatiable longing for more. Even after Bill turned his heart toward me, I yearned for more than he or anyone else could give in this life. In many ways I am more lonely than ever, just because I have tasted the sweetness of intimacy with God and with a man of openhearted candor whom I love. I want to possess this God and this man, but the nature of true love excludes the possessing of so valuable a treasure.

It is excruciating that I only experience that intimacy in snatches, and even the snatches are utterly beyond my control. Those luminous moments with God and the ones I love defy my every effort to manage them. They happen when I least expect or deserve them—not when I'm being good or spiritual or kind or sexy. I simply cannot make them happen by being or doing *anything*. Their very unexpectedness reminds me that I am loved for no discernible reason—like Bill telling me I'm beautiful when I've just confided in him some awful secret about myself and my eyes are swollen from tears. I cherish the shining moments, though they leave me bereft when they pass.

These inexplicable tendernesses undo me. As Gerald May said, "Grace threatens all my normalities."[5] The normal I can predict, prepare for, manage. But grace is out of control. It eludes even as it beckons. I can receive but not command it. I can enjoy but not prolong it. It blesses me with its fierceness and makes me desperate for more, but it offers no guarantee I will experience it again. I cannot plan it, program it, or package it to savor later. I want to extend those grace moments or save them for a rainy day—to cheer me when I'm depressed or lonely or angry. But they don't stay and are never enough and can't be reproduced at will.

Once we've tasted grace living, nothing else will satisfy. My loneliness is the more exquisite for my having been touched by so wonderful a love. I am spoiled for any other lover because I've been loved well. Having been surprised by joy, I am at times profoundly disappointed by the ordinary.

This is what it costs to come alive, to move from the bondage of self-preoccupied codependency to the bonding of our hearts and souls to God and other people. It's not safe, but it's good. It's not easy or comfortable, but it's decidedly worth the effort.

T. S. Eliot, in a classic understatement of the reaction of one of the Magi to finding the Christ after his torturous journey to Bethlehem, concluded: "It was (you may say) satisfactory."[6] The wise man then had to return from his "satisfactory" celebration of the Birth to his ordinary life, lamenting:

> We returned to our places, these Kingdoms,
> But no longer at ease here, in the old dispensation,
> With an alien people clutching their gods.

We, too, live in the midst of an increasingly alien culture where the gods of addiction and codependency are not just clutched but perversely celebrated. We don't fit here any more; our taste of bonding has made us unfit for bondage, and our sacrificial loving has set us apart as odd in our me-centered world.

RECOVERY'S PARADOXES

Yet recovery is ambiguous and relapses inevitable. Though our "satisfactory" experiences of divine and human grace seduce us relentlessly to the arduous trek Home, we're not always sure we want to be on a wilderness journey. The Egypt house of our codependent bondage often looks better to us than the terrifying freedom of choices and surrender to God. We are, at heart, all grumbling Israelites, railing against what is uncomfortable, unfamiliar, risky aliveness. We'd really rather stay enslaved to our self-sufficient mechanisms than live dependent on God alone to take our next step. We fear genuine freedom with all its responsibilities for grace-based, love-dominated living; it feels more normal to be persecuted, hating those who keep us in bondage. Our desert trek is rife with hazards we never dreamed of while safe in the Egypt of our codependency. Loneliness, helplessness, loss of attachments—all our worst fears are realized in the wilderness of our recovery journey.

And it is in the desert that our deep-seated anger against God most clearly reveals itself. In Egypt we could blame Pharaoh and the oppressive taskmasters and the corrupt system. But in the desert we must rail against God if we're unhappy with our loss of predictability and control. There it is clearly *His* hand that is withholding the onions and garlic of Egypt, while offering only the manna of His presence. It's *His* fault we're either stationary for six months (stuck in our "no progress" zone) or frantic for three weeks (everything caving in at once). In the desert our fists go up and we call God cruel for delivering us from codependency. "Thanks, but no thanks," we snarl at Him.

Then He comes to us again in His shining brightness and His compassion, offering us grace for our recovery relapse. It's never a question of whether or not God still loves us. His grace always flows in our direction, uninterrupted, sweet, ready to embrace who we deeply are as soon as we turn back toward Him. It is we who interrupt the flow, who choose our addictions over His grace, who act on fear not faith, who deaden our souls by medicating our pain instead of walking through the pain, our hand in His. We hold the power to choose life or death, and the grace of it all is that the more we choose life, the more our addictions show themselves for what they really are—death-bound strategies that can never deliver the delight or satisfaction they promise.

God shows His faithfulness to us time and again by awakening our longing for the Promised Land where the delight of living in homes we haven't built and enjoying food we haven't planted will be fully ours forever. Like Moses we are captured ever anew by God's majesty and His goodness, and we find ourselves pleading to see His face with our own eyes. And like Moses, we also intercede with the Father on behalf of those we're committed to love. It is, after all, our redeemed nature to love God and others, to trust His grace and to offer it gladly to each other.

Our culture will consider us weird, but John the Beloved assures us recovering codependents with these words: "How great is the love the Father has lavished on us, that we should be called children of God! And that is what we are! The reason the world does not know us is that it did not know him. Dear friends, now we are children of God, and what we will be has not yet been made known. But we know that when he appears, we shall be like him, for we shall see him as he is" (1 John 3:1-2). *For the hope set before us, we can endure the shame of our restoration process.*

Until Home, as we wander (sometimes aimlessly, it seems), through the desert of our recovery, God has promised to grace us with the joy of His forgiveness, wonderful tastes of freedom through His Life in us, and the comfort of His Presence in every sorrow. He calls us to offer that same grace to others as well, then gives us the power to do so. The journey from bondage to bonding is a journey into our Father's endless embrace.

QUESTIONS FOR BUILDING COMMUNITY

1. In a sentence, what is the significance of the phrase "from bondage to bonding"?
2. How is AA's Step Twelve conducive to mutual interdependence?
3. Under what circumstances might you pursue rebonding with your parents?
4. Why must addiction and/or codependency be addressed before mutual interdependence is possible?
5. What limits might a recovering codependent place on his or her relationships that would be consistent with biblical love?
6. Give specific examples from your own life of the cost of bonding in each area:
   a. Willingness to risk.
   b. Choosing to suffer.
7. How is Christlike suffering different from codependent victimization?
8. How can you "carry the message" of your recovery to others in your community? In your church? In your family?

NOTES

1. David A. Seamands, *Healing Grace* (Wheaton, IL: Scripture Press Publications, 1988), page 183.
2. Margery Williams, *The Velveteen Rabbit* (New York: Doubleday & Company, Inc.).
3. Gerald G. May, *Addiction and Grace* (San Francisco, CA: Harper & Row, Publishers, 1988), pages 128-130.
4. John Shea, quoted in *Christianity Today*, April 23, 1990, page 33.
5. May, page 127.
6. T. S. Eliot, "Journey of the Magi," *The Waste Land and Other Poems* (San Diego, CA: Harcourt Brace Jovanovich Publishers, 1958), page 70.
7. Eliot, page 70.

If you benefited from the life-changing message of *From Bondage to Bonding*,
you'll appreciate these titles as well:

THE WOUNDED HEART WORKBOOK.

Now *The Wounded Heart* is available as an in-depth workbook. Designed for individual or group
use, this companion guide will help you deal with the rage, fear, and confusion locked deep
within your soul; provide the guidance you'll need to move into the recovery process; and show
you how to apply specific portions of God's truth to the injured parts of your being.
The Wounded Heart: A Companion Workbook for Personal or Group Use
by Dr. Dan Allender (Oversized Paperback, ISBN 0891096655) $15.00

BOLD LOVE.

We've come to view love and forgiveness as little more than acting pleasantly,
yielding to the will of others, and ignoring offenses. But this definition doesn't begin to
approach the radically disruptive nature of genuine love as set forth by Jesus Christ.
In *Bold Love*, Dr. Dan Allender undermines our comfortable notions of love by drawing out its full,
unrelenting, passionate power. "Bold love is anything but passive," writes Dr. Allender. "It is shrewd,
cunning, and courageous. And in the end it offers not only the promise of genuine reconciliation, but
the ultimate joy of working in partnership with God to surprise and destroy evil in our world."
Bold Love, by Dr. Dan Allender & Dr. Tremper Longman III (Hardcover, ISBN 0891096795) $18.00
Bold Love Group Discussion Guide (Paperback, ISBN 0891096817) $5.00
Bold Love Audio Tape (Includes two 90-minute cassette tapes; SPCN 7900730567) $13.00

INSIDE OUT.

There's more to authentic Christian living than going to church, reading the Bible, teaching Sunday
School, or being nice. Rather, it has to do with facing the realities of your own internal life—the habits,
weaknesses, or personal problems you can't quite shake, the relationships that never seem to work,
the desires that remain unfulfilled—and letting God mold you into a person who is free to be honest,
courageous, and loving. Real change is possible—if you're willing to start from the *Inside Out.*
Inside Out, by Dr. Larry Crabb (Paperback, ISBN 0891096434) $10.00
Inside Out Discussion Guide (Paperback, ISBN 0891092811) $6.00
Inside Out Small Group Video Series (Includes four 45-minute video cassettes,
and a viewer's guide; SPCN 9900735927) $159.00

SILENT PAIN.

What happens when you view God as merely tolerant of your distress rather than
deeply sympathetic? *Silent Pain* speaks to this issue, helping you realize that there's more to
the Christian life than grinning and bearing it. By treating your mind and heart to new
perspectives on God's character, the author explores how mourning allows you to deeply
experience God's tender mercy and a return to peace—with God and with yourself.
Silent Pain: How to Experience the Healing Touch of God's Compassion
by Kathy Olsen (Paperback, ISBN 0891096590) $10.00

Available at your local bookstore, or call (800) 366-7788.

NAVPRESS
BRINGING TRUTH TO LIFE